Refugees in Britain

Refugees in Britain

Practices of Hospitality and Labelling

GILLIAN McFADYEN

EDINBURGH
University Press

Edinburgh University Press is one of the leading university presses in the UK. We publish academic books and journals in our selected subject areas across the humanities and social sciences, combining cutting-edge scholarship with high editorial and production values to produce academic works of lasting importance. For more information visit our website: edinburghuniversitypress.com

First published in hardback by Edinburgh University Press 2020

Edinburgh University Press Ltd
The Tun – Holyrood Road, 12(2f) Jackson's Entry, Edinburgh EH8 8PJ

Typeset in 10/13 ITC Giovanni Std by
IDSUK (DataConnection) Ltd

A CIP record for this book is available from the British Library

ISBN 978 1 4744 4716 4 (hardback)
ISBN 978 1 4744 4717 1 (paperback)
ISBN 978 1 4744 4718 8 (webready PDF)
ISBN 978 1 4744 4719 5 (epub)

CONTENTS

ACKNOWLEDGEMENTS

In developing a project such as this there is always a community of support that goes into it, and this book was definitely not written in isolation. First, I would like to thank all the interviewees who took the time to speak with me, sharing their passion and commitment to refugee welcome. I conducted most of the interviews in 2018, and it really was a 'summer of welcome'. I would also like to extend a massive thank you to BISA for the BISA Early Career Small Research Grant (2018), which allowed me to conduct my research trips.

The project developed from one chapter of my thesis, which I started back in 2010. I would like to acknowledge all the support and guidance I have received from a number of people over the years to get to this stage, including: Jenny Edkins, Patrick Finney, Ayla Gol, Andrew Linklater, Milja Kurki, Lucy Taylor, Berit Bliesemann de Guevara, Catrin Wyn Edwards, Laura Considine, Andrew Davenport, Alistair Shepherd, Birgit Poopuu, Katarzyna Kaczmarska and Andrea Warnecke. Each person has advised, guided and supported me in various ways throughout this project, and I am so grateful.

Finally, I would like to acknowledge the unwavering support of Anna and William McFadyen, and particularly Neil Waghorn. You have been there since the start, and made sure I got to the finish line – thank you.

Introduction

Nestled between the Republic of Malta and Tunisia, the Isle of Lampedusa sits south of the southernmost part of Italy and seventy miles off the coast of Tunisia. Since 2000, the island has experienced several episodes of large scale influxes of people arriving from the African continent (Council of Europe 2011). However, it was in 2013 that Lampedusa started to hit the international news, as it became a hotspot for entry into the European Union. On 3 October 2013, a boat carrying an estimated 500 people, mainly Eritreans, left Libya and capsized claiming 359 lives, in what was the start of a large scale crisis unfolding in the Mediterranean (BBC News 2013). The island again hit the headlines when on 12 April 2015, 400 people on a boat launched from Libya drowned off the coast; 19 April saw 650 people drowning when their boat capsized south of Lampedusa; and a day later, on 20 April, 800 people drowned in the largest recorded Mediterranean shipwreck (BBC News 2015a). In the space of a week, approximately 1,600 people had perished trying to reach Europe. As 2015 progressed, there would be over 1 million sea crossings, starting with the southern Mediterranean routes, but with the intensifying conflict in Syria a new hot spot emerged in the Aegean sea, between Turkey and Greece.

By mid-2015, refugees as a topic were beginning to hit the international press with harrowing accounts emerging. The media documented the movement of individuals in and around the European Union, reporting on shipwrecks, drowning and mass deaths as well as conveying the images of individuals walking along newly erected borders in Hungary, seeking access to the European Union. At the same time though, there were increases in flows from the southern Mediterranean. The movement of refugees and migrants from states such as Eritrea, Sudan, Ethiopia and Somalia led to mass tragedies unfolding in the Mediterranean, whilst all the while the European Union struggled to grapple with the scale and enormity of the situation on its doorstep. Instead, the European Union has implemented policies of border controls, focusing on what it termed pull-factors – factors viewed as encouraging individuals to make such journeys (Mediterranean Migration Research Project).

Indeed, the terms 'refugee crisis', employed throughout this research, and the label 'Mediterranean crisis' – to indicate the period since 2015 that has seen increased movement of people into the European Union, but significantly also increased deterrent policies by states, seeking to prevent access – are not in reference to a crisis of refugees but rather a political crisis. The crisis that was unfolding in the summer of 2015 was not simply a Syrian crisis; there were, and still are, multiple emergencies happening across all continents (Macleod 2016), with a (what should be noted as a small) convergence in the Mediterranean. The movement witnessed in Europe is a mere fraction of the global refugee population of 65 million people of concern (UNHCR). This is not to argue though that this is a 'global refugee crisis': far from it, as most refugees only cross one international border, residing in states such as Turkey, Pakistan, Jordan, Lebanon or Bangladesh (Amnesty International n.d.). But, there has been a gathering of refugee trajectories within the Mediterranean that has led to a heightened situation emerging within this region. As such, the term refugee crisis itself is not actually referring to a crisis of refugees, but rather a political crisis of how the refugees have been handled at the European level, so in this regard, it is a crisis of the refugee, or what Alison Phipps (2019) refers to as a 'reception crisis'.

By late summer of 2015, there was a continuing escalation in media coverage of events within Europe, with incidents such as the suffocation of seventy-one Syrian asylum seekers in an abandoned refrigerated lorry in Austria now making international news (Al Jazeera 2015a). Yet there was still little social or political regard for the situation within Britain. That changed on 7 September 2015 when there was a sudden outpouring of grief, shock, solidarity and support within the Mediterranean crisis, spurred specifically by social media and #RefugeesWelcome and #SolidarityforRefugees that garnered mass coverage both in Britain and abroad. This correlated with images emerging of a young child, Alan Kurdi, who had drowned when his family attempted to cross the Aegean sea. The images were front page news and sparked a massive grassroots reaction, specifically in Britain but also across other European states, that directly challenged the restrictive state response witnessed. Individuals felt compelled to react, and this reaction manifested in multiple ways that I will explore as hospitality.

The British state approach to refugees has been classed as 'paradoxical' (Gibney 2014), placing the refugee at once both in a humanitarian but also a hazardous position as one who threatens the economic security of the state. Consecutive governments since 1990 have been open to providing sanctuary to the refugee based upon Article I. A (2) of the 1951 Convention and Protocol Relating to the Status of Refugees (here on in referred to as the 1951 Convention). Article 1. A. (2) states that a refugee is an individual who can apply for asylum 'owing to a well-founded fear of being persecuted for reasons of race, religion, nationality, membership of a particularly social group, or political opinion' and who is seeking to attain refugee status (UNHCR).

The 1951 Convention defines who is, or is not, a refugee and thus determines who will receive the various entitlements preserved within the Convention. The 1951 Convention definition states that protection is reserved only for those who have left their country of origin. Accordingly, an individual deciding to cross an international border undergoes a transformation into an object of concern under international refugee law, for that individual is missing or has been denied protection in their country of origin and is in need of alternative sources of protection (Helton 2003: 30). Attainment of refugee status then allows individuals who have fled their country to attain sanctuary and the possibility of establishing a new life within their host country. Yet the refugee definition in the 1951 Convention is inherently flexible, allowing states to define for themselves how it should be applied and upheld.

Accordingly, Britain has been offering refuge under specific terms and conditions, due to concerns that the refugee, the guest, is in fact, abusing their welcome. Policies have emerged that have adopted the approach of deterrence and increased border controls in the quest to reduce 'abuse' of the system. One outcome of this has been the creation by consecutive governments of an idealised 'genuine' refugee – an individual with particular experiences, who adheres to certain modes of travel and who is knowledgeable of the national asylum rules; this is offset by the 'bogus' asylum seeker – an individual who is perceived to be abusing the system for economic reasons. This has resulted in a fractured hierarchy of 'refugeehood' in Britain that has allowed consecutive governments to pinpoint, through legislation, exactly who it is who qualifies as a genuine or a bogus refugee. Individuals who fail to meet the criteria are labelled as failed, bogus, asylum seekers or more recently, economic migrants – a label that has grown in prominence since 2015 with the Mediterranean crisis.

This book is a theoretically informed empirical examination of British refugee practices. The ethos of the book is to examine the role and figure of the refugee as situated in British refugee policy. The core argument centres on the complexity and contingency of British refugee policies and politics, what I refer to as hospitality, and its operation with, and through the politics of labelling and externalisation in order to both control and exclude the refugee. British practices of refuge are so constrained and negated that practices of hospitality are geographically positioned far beyond the territorial location of the British state, in order to minimise and contain but, crucially, uphold hospitality. It is still present, but under extreme conditions whereby in fact what I call hostipitality is practised. Within hospitality, the British state, in order to protect the practices of hospitality from the 'parasitical guest' can go as far as to cease partaking in the act of hospitality altogether. I argue that through the politics of labelling, the refugee and practices of hospitality are geographically externalised beyond Britain and the EU itself, and located purely in the camps surrounding Syria. In this aspect, the monograph proposes that what we have witnessed within the British approach to the Mediterranean crisis is a practice of hospitality grounded in humanitarianism that is geographically externalised beyond the state, in order to uphold the

British values of humanitarianism, whilst at the same time deterring, containing and preventing refugees. The monograph also engages with counter-discourses, or what could be viewed as counter-ethics, by examining local, community practices of British hospitality, showing the acts of solidarity and hospitality that challenge the statist logic.

In doing so, I examine the British refugee system in two distinct areas. I begin, first, by offering a distinct theoretical discussion on the practices of hospitality and of labelling in order to build a framework to apply throughout the empirical examination, but also a theoretical framework that can be informed and challenged by the empirics. Hospitality is the key concept deployed here. This is a principle that implies 'the right of the stranger not to be treated with hostility when he arrives at someone else's territory' (Derrida 2000: 4). This approach instils the state, the host, with a level of power to wield against the refugee guest, by dictating the terms of hospitality; in extreme cases, the state will preserve the dignity of the institution itself by ceasing the practice of hospitality altogether. According to this principle, all should be welcomed and allowed to put forth a claim for refuge, for to open our house to the unknown stranger and provide them with shelter and sanctuary without asking for anything in return is the essence of hospitality. For, as Heidrun Friese (2010: 327) acknowledges, hospitality 'grounded in human sociability as well as in human vulnerability and finitude, is not a "virtue", a sort of kindness or benevolence, but a right'. Yet, as Emmanuel Levinas asserted, to welcome the other raised questions of 'our freedom, our security, our vulnerability, however justified' (cited in Derrida 1999a: 29). In engaging with hospitality, the book seeks to develop the approach beyond Derrida, and develop an understanding of hospitality as externalised humanitarianism whereby hospitality is projected beyond the territorial confines of the state, thereby creating a framework that can be employed throughout the research to examine and analyse the British response to refugees, be it historically or especially in relation to the Mediterranean crisis.

In addition to hospitality, the politics of labelling is also drawn upon. This is a theoretical approach that has, as yet, not been analysed in conjunction with hospitality. Labelling is traditionally drawn from the fields of refugee studies and development theory, but is an approach that focuses on the value, identification and power behind labels. Labels are inherently political by nature and do not emerge from a political vacuum. In the unequal relationship between the refugee and the host, it is the state that is doing the labelling, for the labeller is in a position of power, determining who is to be included or excluded. As such, the framework helps to assist and strengthen the application of hospitality throughout the research, for central to labelling are the processes of categorisation and identification – conditional aspects of hospitality where one needs to know the other. By employing the politics of labelling alongside hospitality the book examines novel ways of identifying new values, power relations and dynamics within the theory of hospitality. In addition, the research looks to develop a new understanding of hospitality, that of an externalised humanitarian hospitality whereby the practice is geographically projected beyond the territorial confines of the state as a means to uphold and curtail the practice simultaneously. Labelling is a central practice that, I argue, facilitates the externalisation of hospitality.

The second part of the research presents three case studies: British internal asylum policies (1990–2018), British external policies during the Mediterranean crisis (2010–18) and finally, a counter-analysis of hospitality practices at the British local level (2015–18), examining grassroots organisations practising hospitality in response to the Mediterranean crisis. The research provides detailed and original research into the British approach to refuge, offering a unique multi-layered approach, be it the local, state or regional level. In doing so, I examine internal and external practices of hospitality and labelling and how they have been wielded by the British state. I do this through examining how British refugee politics have constructed an idealised genuine refugee figure, as well as how Britain has employed practices of humanitarian externalisation and geographical exclusion in response to the Mediterranean crisis. This is where humanitarian principles are espoused whilst at the same time being entrenched in language of deterrence, security, risk and containment, and the refugee (and refugee policy) is positioned, or contained, beyond the sphere of Britain or the European Union (Betts and Milner 2007).

Empirically, the research employs an enriched mixed-methods approach to complement the theoretical framework. Thirty-four semi-structured interviews were conducted in five locations – London, Cardiff, Manchester, Birmingham and mid-Wales towns (Aberystwyth, Machynlleth and Newtown) – over the period from November 2017 to September 2018. The sites of research were selected due to the hub of activities that developed during the summer of 2015, whereas the more local towns in Wales were identified in order to show the reach and extent of hospitality that was practised during the same period. My approach to the interviews followed what John Van Maanen and Deborah Kolb (cited in Bryman 2008: 296) refer to as 'not a matter to be taken lightly, but one that involves some combination of strategic planning, hard work and dumb luck'. The focus was on targeting refugee groups that were established in mid-2015 in direct response to events witnessed in the Mediterranean crisis, as well as individuals (activists, refugee policy advisers, lawyers and day-to-day citizens) who became mobilised during this period. The individual response varied considerably, from individuals who opened up their homes in a direct act of hospitality or set up Community Sponsorship programmes to the offering of food and clothing and providing hospitality practices within Britain via foodbanks, outreach, charity support and welcome centres. But there were also those who externalised their practices of hospitality beyond the British state, extending their hospitality to camps within France and Greece, providing security, food, clothing and assistance. The interviews are primarily utilised in Chapter 5 and provide a counter-discourse to the state approach – one that is grounded in the politics of inclusion, solidarity, welcome and hospitality.

In addition to the research interviews, the monograph draws on substantial archival material, specifically the Hansard parliamentary archive, where an intense twenty-eight year period of parliamentary debates (from 1990 to 2018) has been examined, to chart the response to refugee movements. The focus of the archival work was to ascertain how successive governments have sought to define an idealised notion of a genuine asylum seeker through the use of labelling and its implementation in subsequent policies, as well as to examine the framing of the Mediterranean crisis by politicians from 2010 to 2018. This material is primarily employed within Chapters 3 and Chapter 4 to inform discussions of the British response to refugees, both domestically and during the Mediterranean crisis.

Chapter Overview

Chapter 1 introduces the theoretical framework of hospitality – a principle developed by Jacques Derrida. The chapter examines how we engage with and position the other when they enter our milieu. By employing hospitality, a state must be willing to open its border to all those who seek sanctuary. It asks us to open our house to the unknown stranger and provide them with shelter and sanctuary without asking for anything in return. Yet, this is where the paradox of hospitality emerges, with conditional hospitality evolving. Hospitality should be open to all who seek it yet at the same time the notion of unconditional hospitality needs to be, and can only be, conditional. This chapter addresses the framework of both conditional and unconditional hospitality before then examining the notion of hostipitality. For Derrida (2000: 3), hospitality is 'parasitized by its opposite, "hostility," the undesirable guest [hôte] which it harbours as the self-contradiction in its own body'. The chapter seeks to develop beyond Derrida, drawing inspiration from work by writers such as Mireille Rosello (2001), Judith Still (2013) and Dan Bulley (2017), to present a broad critical hospitality that is less structured than Derrida's approach. I use these approaches of hospitality to develop the framework further towards what I term an externalised hospitality of humanitarianism, by means of which a state such as Britain is capable of geographically projecting hospitality far beyond its territorial confines.

Chapter Two introduces the politics of labelling to explore an approach that examines how labelling shapes, defines and castigates the other into particular power hierarchies. Labelling does not occur within a political vacuum. The creation and application of labels is always political, and it is crucial to remember that words matter – labels matter – and how we label someone impacts not only on their position but also on our interactions and responsibilities towards them. As Geof Woods acknowledges, labelling 'is a relationship of power, asymmetrical and one-sided' (Wood 1985). Drawing upon the work of Roger Zetter, Howard Becker, Michel Foucault and Geof Wood, through the politics of labelling we are able to witness the fear of the perceived abusive other that emerges through conditional hospitality. Indeed, we can examine how the fear of the abusive other leads to the state establishing multiple labels of inferiority in order to protect the right to refuge from the perceived abused. Accordingly, the politicisation of labelling allows the government to determine the level of hospitality directed towards the refugees in question. With the fracturing of the refugee label, individuals are increasingly unable to attain the label refugee or asylum seeker, and instead fall into subsequent inferior categorisations, thus inferring hostipitality from the state.

Chapter 2 thus identifies and asserts the importance of labelling and how it occurs for the benefit of politicians and governments to control, regulate and monitor asylum flows, particularly when offering conditional hospitality. The politics of labelling establishes hierarchies of need that feed into hostipitality. In examining the politics of labelling, the chapter begins by examining three prominent approaches to labelling, from Roger Zetter, Howard Becker and Michel Foucault, examining the value and significance of labelling. The chapter then examines the politics of labelling, focusing on its implications, before examining the exclusionary politics of labelling the other. It finishes by turning the focus of examination from the labelled to the labeller, looking at the power and the distance that come from being in the privileged position. This examination highlights the processes involved in labelling, examining the power dynamics that can emerge and how certain labels evolve that position, categorise and castigate the refugee. Finally, the chapter examines the emergence of highly politicised labels as well as the process of fragmentation or fractioning of labels into sub-categories of reduced political value.

Chapter 3 draws upon both the politics of labelling and practices of hostipitality in order to address how British governments have constructed a genuine asylum seeker. Since 1990, when Britain witnessed a spike in asylum applications, consecutive governments have adopted a stance towards refuge whereby the interests of the state supersede those of people seeking asylum. By employing

Derrida and the politics of labelling, Chapter 3 addresses how the politics of hospitality and labelling operate in the state's interest and at the expense of the refugee. The chapter identifies five ways in which Conservative (1990–7), New Labour (1997–2010), Conservative Liberal Democratic coalition (2010–15) governments have sought to establish the label of a genuine refugee.

Drawing upon the language and framing of the refugee from Hansard parliamentary archives since 1990, Chapter 3 presents a narrative of an idealised figure of refuge that has been constructed through consecutive governments, at the expense of the refugee, with the end product being a tangible, one-size-fits-all figure of a genuine asylum seeker. This figure is upheld as honourable, legal and legitimate. The chapter argues that therefore what we are witnessing within the British asylum system is the politics of hostipitality, with hostility being the overriding reaction to the asylum seeker. The chapter draws on Hansard Parliamentary debates, speeches and written communication both within the House of Commons and the House of Lords since 1990, examining the Conservative government from 1990 to 1997, New Labour (1997–2010) and the Conservative and Liberal Democrats coalition government (2010–15), using the terms 'asylum seeker', 'refugee' and 'immigrant'. The chapter then concludes with an analysis of the 2018 Windrush scandal, examining the state policies of hospitality at play. I argue that the framework of the hostile environment, developed overtly since 2012, has much deeper political routes within the British refugee system and the Windrush scandal was an overt manifestation of the politics of hospitality, facilitated by the re-labelling of a designated group within society from citizen to non-citizen.

Chapter 4 presents the case of the Mediterranean crisis and the British response. The chapter addresses the politics of hospitality and labelling, and examines how British responsibility has been geographically externalised beyond Britain and the EU. This chapter offers an analysis of the labels used to define the people displaced in the Mediterranean refugee crisis and discusses the politics behind the labelling. In doing so, it intertwines the politics of externalisation beyond the EU and highlights the practice of containment that is perceived as the moral response to the crisis, thus showing British responsibility as one of humanitarianism rather than of hospitality. Responsibility is geographically externalised, beyond the EU, rather than on British shores. Accordingly, the chapter addresses firstly, the politics of labelling operating within the Mediterranean crisis. It then examines the geographical relations of the refugee, focusing on the significance of the camps for the British response. The chapter then finishes with a focus on the theory of distant suffering (Boltanski 1999) and how distance and moral responsibility operates within the British approach to the Mediterranean crisis. The overall emphasis is on how language and labelling are employed in order to geographically frame and conceptualise the Mediterranean crisis and externalise the British (humanitarian) response, beyond the sphere of Europe. Through drawing a demarcating line between those internal and external to the EU, the Conservative government have been able to establish a narrative of humanitarianism that is rooted solely in the camps, in and surrounding Syria.

The final chapter offers a counter-discourse case study to the previous state understanding of hospitality by focusing on the practice of hospitality that emerged at the grassroots, community level during the summer of 2015 in Britain in direct response to state inaction during the Mediterranean crisis. Chapter 5 identifies practices of hospitality employed by local actors within Britain, operating at the internal level but also externally, being geographically projected beyond the territorial confines of the state. As noted, the chapter is founded on interviews from thirty-four activists and aims to develop a counter understanding of hospitality, one that is inherently grounded in welcome, solidarity and support. The chapter examines the significance of the Mediterranean crisis and the geographical closeness of this crisis as a means for activist engagement. It then examines the myriad activities employed internally before examining the emergence and significance of Community Sponsorship programmes. A discussion on external practices of hospitality is then provided, and the chapter concludes with an examination of hospitality as resistance, for hospitality is perceived by many activists as a moral, or ethical stand against state inaction. The chapter will operate as a critique of the state-centred hostipitality, presenting a grassroots movement attuned to responsibility and counter-ethics of unconditional hospitality against the statist approach.

This book offers a novel way of looking at British refugee politics, arguing that the British approach is one grounded in politics of hospitality – a hospitality that for years now has been presented as being abused by the bogus guest. In order to maintain and preserve hospitality, Britain has intensified the processes of refuge, implementing stricter policies and guidelines that have to be met, thus maintaining a humanitarian facade whilst curtailing and containing the refugee other. This process, I argue, intensified during the Mediterranean crisis, with the focus on the refugee external to Britain and the EU. The British response of hospitality, facilitated by the politics of labelling, allows for humanitarian concerns still to exist, but purely through an externalised lens. What are called into question through this analysis of hospitality and the politics of labelling are the geographical hierarchies of need that emerge in response to the Mediterranean crisis. Through labelling, the refugee is geographically projected beyond Britain and the EU, with those internal to the EU transformed into (illegal) economic migrants, thus negating British responsibility.

CHAPTER 1

Hospitality, Hostility, Hostipitality

In his essay 'Perpetual peace', Immanuel Kant (1795) described hospitality as

> the Right of a stranger in consequence of his arrival on the soil of another country, not to be treated by its citizens as an enemy when he arrives in the land of another ... One may refuse to receive him when this can be done without causing his destruction; but, so long as he peacefully occupies his place, one may not treat him with hostility

Kant spoke of hospitality as an 'eternal peace', a universal hospitality without limit that we each inhibit by 'virtue of our common possession of the surface of the earth, where, as a globe, they cannot indefinitely disperse and hence must finally tolerate the presence of each other'. Through our common ownership of the earth, Kant (1795) was arguing that there then is a universal right to hospitality, acting as a tonic for the violence and hostility within the world, leading to a 'perpetual peace among nations'.

I want to turn this analysis first towards the theory of hospitality, and how this notion can be employed to understand the positioning of the contemporary refugee. Through engaging with hospitality, particularly the work of Jacques Derrida, I want to examine the notion of hospitality, and argue how hospitality is not only (and can only be) conditional, but has been marginalised, with hostility towards the refugee becoming the main driving force of government policies and debates. In short, this is a chapter that focuses on exploring hospitality and draws on Derrida, but it is not a chapter on Derrida. The intention is to engage with Derrida, but go beyond him in order to stretch and develop the concept of hospitality, in the vein of Mireille Rosello (2001), Judith Still (2013) and Dan Bulley (2017).

To do so, I offer an introduction to the concepts of unconditional and conditional hospitality, before focusing more closely on hospitality and the parasitical guest, xenophobia and the politics of hostipitality. The chapter will then conclude by seeking to stretch the term of hospitality to develop a new understanding of hospitality as that of externalised humanitarian hospitality. This is a hospitality that is projected beyond the territory of a state as a means to verify conditionality. Hospitality need not be confined by the territorial boundaries of a state and can be externalised as a means to control and protect the practice of hospitality. I argue that this a distinct feature of contemporary British refugee policy, where hostility and projected humanitarian hospitality are in practice.

The Ethical Question of Hospitality

Through his works *Of Hospitality* (2000) and *On Cosmopolitanism and Forgiveness* (2001), Derrida (1993: 8) provides a notion of hospitality he describes as unconditional, absolute or pure and asserts is the 'essence of culture'. For hospitality 'inevitably touches on that fundamental ethical question (since it is itself an ethical foundation) of the boundaries of the human, and how we set these up' (Still 2013: 4). In this aspect, hospitality is not simply 'one ethic amongst others' (Derrida 2001: 16); rather, as Derrida (1993: 50) asserts, hospitality is ethics – hospitality 'is the whole and the principle of ethics'. In a simple manner, Derrida (1997) understood hospitality 'as a very general name for all our relations to the other'. Unconditional hospitality posits that hospitality should be open to all who seek it. That the *hôte* [host] provides the stranger with the gift of being 'at home . . . that is given by a hospitality more ancient than the inhabitant himself' (1993: 10). In providing hospitality to the unknown stranger, Derrida views it as the 'crossing of the threshold by the guest who must be at once called, desired, and expected, but also always free to come or not to come. It is indeed a question of admitting, accepting, and inviting'. Of inviting the stranger, the unknown other, or what Derrida (1993: 34) refers to as

> The *arrivant*, who is not even a guest. He surprises the host – who is not yet a host or an inviting power – enough to call into question, to the point of annihilating or rendering indeterminate, all the distinctive signs of a prior identity, beginning with the very border that delineated a legitimate home.

When a refugee arrives at a state, they cross over a border, a threshold, without an invitation, and ask for asylum. The principle of refuge 'creates the desire for a welcome without reserve and without calculation, an exposure without limit to whoever arrives' (Derrida 2005a: 6). According to Derrida, all should be welcomed. He notes, 'I have to welcome the other, whoever he or she is unconditionally, without asking for a document, a name, a context, or a passport' (1997). Derrida (2005b: 67) stresses that the practice of unconditional or pure hospitality means that you do not impose conditions on the welcome. The host cannot ask for knowledge or identification. But at the same time

> it also assumes that you address them, individually, and thus that you call them something and grant them a proper name: 'What are you called, you?' Hospitality consists in doing everything possible to address the other, to grant or ask them their name, while avoiding this question becoming a 'condition', a police inquisition, a registration of information, or a straightforward frontier control.

Through his work, Derrida's understanding was that unconditional hospitality implies that the host does not question the guest, for the guest does not need to provide any answers, nor even identify themselves, or provide anything physical back to the extent that if the stranger denies you your home, you have to acknowledge this as part of the hospitality (Derrida 2000). For the concept of unconditional hospitality requires us to open our house to the stranger, to the 'absolute, unknown anonymous other' and provide them with shelter and sanctuary without asking for anything in return

(Derrida 2000: 25). When Derrida (1997) speaks on the necessity of hospitality, he has in mind the need to

> not simply assimilate the other . . . We have to welcome the Other inside – without that there would be no hospitality, that the Other should be sheltered or welcomed in my space, and I should try to open my space, without trying to include the Other in my space.

Erin Wilson (2010: 111) reminds us that hospitality 'is not simply a legal, technical, dispassionate undertaking but a relationship that requires compassion, understanding and generosity'. Indeed, through unconditional hospitality, Derrida reminds us that the host should respect the singularity of the other and not ask him or her that he respect or keep intact the host's own space or culture. The concept of hospitality requires a recognition and respect for the stranger seeking sanctuary. The notion of hospitality 'implies an understanding that we are not all the same, but that we respect the differences of others, and enables us to retain our own unique differences whilst opening up a space for the "stranger"' (Goodhall 2010: 6).

In this instance, unconditional hospitality is not a form of inclusion, which Derrida argues is problematic, for it potentially raises issues of equality, assimilation and acceptance that can or could be coerced. Rather, Derrida (1997) proposed:

> I offer unconditional hospitality that the Other may ruin my own space or impose his or her culture or his or her own language. That's the problem: hospitality should be neither assimilation, acculturation, nor simply the occupation of my space by the Other.

Derrida (1999b: 70) acknowledges that this is the risk of hospitality and that this is 'terrible to accept, but that is the condition of unconditional hospitality: that you give up the mastery of your space, your home, your nation. It is unbearable'. Derrida (1997) stressed, 'I have to welcome the other . . . unconditionally . . . I have to keep it open or try to keep it open unconditionally'. In opening yourself to the unknown other, offering them mastery of your home, in being 'unprepared, or prepared to be unprepared, for the unexpected arrival of any other', this is where 'unconditionality is a frightening thing, it's scary' (Derrida 1997). It is this complete openness to the other that introduces the host to the notion of threats, limitations and fear of the stranger (Derrida 2000: 25). For the host is offered no knowledge or history of the other who presents themselves at their door, and cannot ask owing to the unconditionality of hospitality. The arrivant, then, is the unidentifiable other. Derrida (2003: 129) asserts that due to the unconditionality required, 'hospitality, to be sure, is practically impossible to live; one cannot in any case, and by definition, organize it'. To organise and control is to lose the unconditionality.

The Conditionality of Hospitality

By employing hospitality, a state must be willing to open its borders to all those who seek sanctuary. Yet, this is where the paradox within unconditional hospitality appears, with conditional hospitality emerging that then provides a limitation of the notion of hospitality that then takes precedence. Hospitality should be open to all who seek it, yet at the same time, the notion of unconditional hospitality needs to be, and can only be, conditional. For as Derrida (2000: 77) argues, unconditional hospitality, opening your home, allowing the other to cross your threshold without identifying themselves, 'these rights and duties are always conditioned and conditional'. This is the paradox of unconditional hospitality. It seeks to rise above the laws of hospitality, but it fails to detach itself from said laws – this is the double bind that Derrida speaks of (Derrida 1999a: 33). As Derrida (2000: 81) explains, 'they incorporate one another at the moment of excluding one another . . . they are both more or less hospitable, hospitable and inhospitable'. Unconditional hospitality can only be conditional, for in establishing a home, one is automatically erecting a border, demarcating what is inside and outside. In creating a home, you create a space with a border that is yours through a process of inclusion and exclusion. The guest must cross over a border, a threshold, in order to be included, hence the conditionality of the hospitality. Derrida (2000: 14) refers to this as the 'gap' between the hospitality of invitations and the hospitality of visitation. He writes:

> for there to be hospitality, there must be a door. But if there is a door, there is no longer hospitality. There is no hospitable house. There is no house without doors and windows. But as soon as there are a door and windows, it means that someone has the key to them and consequently controls the conditions of hospitality. There must be a threshold. But if there is a threshold, there is no longer hospitality.

In this regard, Derrida (2000: 149) reaffirms his argument that 'pure unconditional hospitality appears inaccessible', for a border always needs to be crossed in entering into a host's house (or state). The host retains possession of the space, be it the house, the nation, the country, but significantly the threshold is still in their control (Derrida 1999b: 69), hence, the inherent paradox of hospitality, as well as its conditionality.

So, how exactly then does conditional hospitality operate? Catherine Brun (2010: 371) notes, in order to provide hospitality, 'one has to have control and ownership of a place. It requires the rights to a particular place, and it involves power and inequality in the relation between the host and the guest.' In this instance, the quest to ascertain if one's guest is genuine or not can place the position of the host on the defensive. Through conditional hospitality, Derrida (2000: 15) notes that the act of seeking hospitality begins with the speaking of the stranger and the utilisation and employment of the host's language in order to ask for and attain sanctuary. This is the first violence against the stranger, having to 'assert their rights' in a foreign language, and Derrida (2005b: 68) argues that it is almost impossible to negate this violence. Conditional hospitality then is the inevitable (political) compromise in the claim for unconditional hospitality and actually allows the host to wield a significant amount of power by placing restrictions on the greeting extended to the guest (Wilson 2010: 113). Yet at the same time, the notion of unconditional hospitality needs to be, and can only be, conditional. It is the negotiation and balance between unconditional and conditional hospitality that makes the concept of hospitality political (Clitchley and Kearney cited in Derrida 2001: x). For how is any state able to cope with the possibility of accepting all who approach its border for sanctuary? Through conditional hospitality, the guest must follow 'our rules, our way of life, even our language, our culture, our political system' (Derrida cited in Borradori 2003: 128). In creating a home, the master creates a space with a border that is his through a process of inclusion and exclusion, 'he controls the borders and when he welcomes the guest he wants to keep the mastery' (Derrida 1999b: 69).

The quest to maintain the mastery of one's home can lead, Derrida argued, to the host questioning if the guest is genuine or not. This questioning can place the host on the defensive with the aim of protecting the practice of hospitality. Accordingly, the right of conditional hospitality raised a question for Derrida regarding the misuse of hospitality. How is one to know that the hospitality that is being provided is not being abused by what Derrida terms 'parasites'? For Derrida (2003: 128) noted that the host accepts 'the foreigner, the other, the foreign body up to a certain point. And so not without restrictions.' For the practice of hospitality means that, for the host, it

> supposes a reception or inclusion of the other which one seeks to appropriate, control, and master according to different modalities of violence, there is a history of hospitality, an always possible perversion of the law of hospitality . . . and of the laws which come to limit and condition it in its inscription as a law. (Derrida 2001: 117)

It is at this stage, as Catherine Brun (2010: 371) notes, that conditional hospitality can be identified as the 'political dimension'. Conditional hospitality places restriction and rules on those who can and cannot attain hospitality, introducing a level of hostility to the process, and as Erin Wilson (2010) asserted, it creates a level of power for the host, creating an unequal relationship between the host and the guest. In this regard, the position of tolerance can be viewed as 'conditional, circumspect, careful hospitality' (Derrida 2003: 128). So, to develop hospitality, it is not inclusion or acceptance, but rather a position of tolerance. Yet tolerance challenges the practices of conditional hospitality. For tolerance is perceived as the opposite of hospitality, or the extreme of hospitality. Through tolerance, the host is able to retain the mastery of their own home: 'because I am tolerant, it is because I wish to limit my welcome, to retain power and maintain control over the limit of my own "home", my sovereignty, my "I can" (my territory, my house, my language, my culture, my religion)' (Derrida 2003: 128). Tolerance in hospitality is a

> kind of condescending concession on the side of the reason of the strongest, it says to the other from its elevated positions 'I am letting you be . . . I am leaving you a place in my home, but do not forget that this is my home!' (Derrida 2003: 127)

In this regard, tolerance can be perceived as a form of 'scrutinized hospitality, always under surveillance, parsimonious and protective of hospitality' (Derrida 2003: 128). As Derrida (1995: 71) reflected on the relation to the other,

> I can respond only to the other (or to the One), that is, to the other, by sacrificing the other to that one. I am responsible to any one (that is to say to any other) only by failing in my responsibilities to all the others, to the ethical or political generality.

Yet this in itself raises questions of the purity of the act of hospitality itself. For 'would a hospitality without risk, a hospitality backed by certain assurances, a hospitality protected by an immune system against the wholly other, be true hospitality' (Derrida 2003: 129). For hospitality is connected to the unknown arrival that cannot be determined. Risk is a central factor for hospitality, regardless if whether it is conditional or unconditional, hence why Derrida (1999b: 70) acknowledged that it was 'unbearable', impractical, unliveable. How can you protect against the potential unknown arrival of a stranger? Tracey Skillington (2016: 101) connects this with the desire of the unknown stranger, asking, 'the question of rights and the possibility of accommodating the stranger become utterly conditional on the degree to which the presence of this stranger is desired'.

'Parasitical' Guests and Hostility

Derrida questioned that not all guests might be genuine and that in itself can lead to fear and suspicion on the part of the host, leading the host to question whether the guest is genuine or what he termed 'parasitical'. Indeed, Derrida (2000: 59) set out the problem between the genuine and the parasitical guest:

> How can we distinguish between a guest and a parasite? In principle, the difference is straightforward, but for that you need a law, hospitality, reception, the welcome offered has to be submitted to a basic and limiting jurisdiction. Not all new arrivals are received as guests if they don't have the benefit of the right to hospitality or the right of asylum etc. Without this right, a new arrival can only be introduced 'in my home', in the hosts 'at home', as a parasite, a guest who is wrong, illegitimate, clandestine, liable to expulsion or arrest.

In order to maintain hospitality only for the genuine guest, hosts can go so far as to become 'virtually xenophobic' in the aim to provide sanctuary only to the those deemed genuine (Derrida 2000: 53). Hospitality, as discussed, is firmly rooted in conditions and practices in order to maintain the host as master, but Derrida (2005a: 5) argues that the host could go as far as to protect their right to offer hospitality to only the genuine by ceasing to partake in the act of hospitality altogether – the host should rally against unlimited hospitality to the other in order to 'render the welcome effective, determined, concrete, to put it into practice'. Ben Jelloun (cited in Still 2013: 27) refers to this as the 'unlearning of hospitality', when he observes that states are constrained by time and limited by space: 'there's a shortage of accessibility, or in other words of generosity and freedom, because everything is calculated and measured. Doors are shut, and so are hearts.' The end result can be a policy of protectionism through the complete suspension of the practice altogether. As Derrida (2000: 53–5) explained:

> One can become virtually xenophobic in order to protect or claim to protect one's own hospitality . . . I want to be master at home . . . to be able to receive whomever I like there. Anyone who encroaches on my 'at home', on my ipseity, on my power of hospitality, on my sovereignty as host, I start to regard as an undesirable foreigner, and virtually as an enemy. This other becomes a hostile subject, and I risk becoming their hostage.

Through suspending the practice, and the fear and suspicion that arises in the practices of hospitality, we are able to witness how hospitality is actually tainted by its exact opposite, hostility, 'the undesirable guest [hôte] which it harbours as the self-contradiction in its own body' (Derrida 2000: 3). As Bonnie Honig (cited in Friese 2010: 324) asserts, 'hospitality harbors a trace of its double-hostility'. Thus, in the words of Derrida (2003: 124), 'a state that closes its borders to noncitizens, monopolizes violence, controls its borders, excludes or represses noncitizens ... Once again the state is both self-protecting and self-destroying, at once remedy and poison.' By removing the risk of hospitality and removing the possibility of the unknown guest arriving, the host suspends the act of hospitality altogether. Unconditional hospitality means accepting risk; accepting the risk and potential fear of the other undermining, challenging or usurping the status quo. The risk of pure, unconditional hospitality is the perpetual fear of the other's motives, which can never be foreseen – it is fear of the unknown (Derrida 1999b: 70). Unconditional hospitality is a process of exposure – of exposing oneself to a myriad potential outcomes that the host cannot predict or respond to in advance. Yet, the fear, the risk or the suspicion continuously undermines the process of hospitality, a factor that appears to be common across Western and central Europe, whereby the risk of the (refugee or migrant) other has become too much of a gamble; this is the risk of Ulrich Beck (2002: 40), where we can understand that 'risk' 'inherently contains the concept of control'. As Derrida (1999b: 70) asserted,

> the newcomer may be a good person, or may be the devil; but if you exclude the possibility that the newcomer is coming to destroy your house – if you want to control this and exclude in advance this possibility – there is no hospitality. In this case, you control the border, you have customs officers, and you have a door, a gate, a key and so on. For unconditional hospitality to take place you have to accept the risk of the other coming and destroying the place, initiating a revolution, stealing everything, or killing everyone. This is the risk of pure hospitality and pure gift, because a pure gift might be terrible too.

And this conditionality of hospitality, highlights clearly the ethics of hospitality, the ethical questions, or responsibility towards the other, whilst highlighting the violence of hospitality, the control of hospitality and the exclusionary nature of hospitality. Conditional hospitality is an expression of 'ethos', for Derrida (2001:17) asserts, 'our way of being, the residence, one's home, the familiar place of dwelling . . . the manner in which we relate to ourselves and to others, to others as our own or as foreigners, ethics is hospitality'. Committing fully to the other, through an ethical relationship, be it conditional or unconditional hospitality, is problematic and unworkable. This is the ethical double bind of hospitality and to the ethics of hospitality is the negotiation between the conditional and the unconditional.

Externalising Hospitality: A Geographical Hierarchy of Humanitarian Hospitality

In engaging with Derrida's hospitality, I want to conclude this chapter by critically challenging the location of hospitality as residing at the state level. Hospitality is traditionally connected with the state, with Derrida discussing the centrality of the state to the ethics of hospitality. Through the construction of the foreign other, the state is bound up within this relationship. The laws of hospitality are 'bound up with the state as sovereign as that which determines laws and duty' (Westmoreland 2008: 4). As Rosello warned, within the twenty-first century, hospitality is positioned at the epicentre of our political, social and economic life for refugees, asylum seekers and immigrants, 'their families, friends, and relatives, immigration officers, political leaders, and the most anonymous of citizens are all affected by the ways in which the state legitimizes some forms of hospitality while declaring others irresponsible, unrealistic, dangerous, or even illegal' (Rosello 2001: 6). I want to develop beyond Derrida and stretch the theory of hospitality, to develop a new understanding to the approach. I seek to draw from Judith Still's (2013) approach to hospitality, that it be 'recognised as a structure with no fixed content'. That it is not connected purely to the territorial confines of a state. In this regard, I posit that hospitality can operate not simply at the state or individual level, or simply within a confines of a state territory, of which Derrida acknowledges himself, but that actually, the practice of hospitality can be mobile.

In developing the approach to hospitality, I argue that the practice of hospitality can be transferable and relocated beyond the confines of the state. Rosello (2001: 69) stresses that one of the central issues when it comes to encounters with the other, particularly beyond our homes, 'when we become strangers in a strange place', is that we are never sure if 'our own models of hospitality are transferable'. The hospitality I am referring to here is a new approach of hospitality that need not be confined to the territory of the nation state but can exist beyond the border. That hospitality need not be tied to the state, but rather can be projected geographically beyond the confines of the state. The state is still the actor wielding hospitality, but it is not the only actor, but as Rosello (2001: 38) stresses,

> the implied consequences of the state's right to interfere in the definition of what constitutes an authorised guest is that the host's house is a subset of the national territory and that private gestures of hospitality are always a subcategory of national hospitality.

Derrida's focus on hospitality is always on the inclusion or exclusion of the other, and the crossing of the threshold, particularly at the sovereign border, but what happens when that threshold is moved and hospitality is no longer bound to the territory of a state? What happens when the threshold is rolled out beyond the territory, externalised and geographically projected far beyond the territory of the host nation state? How does hospitality operate then, and what kind of hospitality is at play? Derrida (2000: 55) argues that 'there is no hospitality without finitude, sovereignty can only be exercised by filtering, choosing, and thus excluding and doing violence'. That violence and injustice begins at the threshold of hospitality, so what happens when that threshold is moved? Does it negate the violence and injustice, or does the repositioning of hospitality further intensify the violence and constitutes the injustice? With the British example, as we will go on to discuss, we have been witnessing the externalisation of hospitality. Alongside the externalisation of hospitality, I argue that there has been an adaptation in hospitality; that it has been externalised, but also that it has been presented as humanitarian hospitality. By externalising hospitality, organisations such as the United Nations High Commissioner for Refugees can intervene within the 'crisis', offering case protection workers who focus on the determination of refugee status, alongside British Home Office case workers. As such, even through externalised hospitality, conditionality is paramount within programmes such as the Vulnerable Persons Resettlement Scheme.

In seeking to understand the projection of hospitality, Erin Wilson (2010: 111) argues that hospitality sees the host regard the stranger who arrives at the threshold and offers a welcome, whilst at the same time offering a welcome to 'those far off who have not yet asked for our help . . . hospitality implies that protection must be offered in the first place unconditionally and to the unnamed, unknown other'. In this regard, the guest resides external to the host, waiting to manifest into a guest. Yet, hospitality can be international, as George Cavallar (2002: 71) reminds us, when it is applied to 'members of "out groups" of different cultures and communities'. Indeed, Cavallar (2002: 3) asserts that 'international hospitality can be interpreted as a means and vehicle to promote the evolution' of a 'juridical commonwealth or of a global civil society based on universal principles or norms', in line with Kant's universal right to hospitality 'as a perpetual peace'. He does argue that through a practice of international hospitality, a commonwealth is developed and upheld at the international level. Whilst upholding that states are the actors of hospitality, they are not the only actors operating the practice of hospitality. As will be analysed in Chapter 5, hospitality can be employed at the community, local level, and can be wielded as resistance. Thus hospitality can be projected beyond the territorial confines of a state, not in order to establish an international commonwealth of hospitality, but rather to further control, curtail and increase the conditionality of hospitality, reifying the risk and threat of the practice. Much in line with Mireille Rosello's (2001) work on hospitality, I argue that hospitality is in crisis, 'not simply because our contemporary (Western?) world may not have enough of it, but because it is in the process of being redefined'. Yet, I would argue, the practice of hospitality is not just being redefined, but also relocated, becoming mobile and externally projected, thus creating further tensions upon the practice that strengthen the conditionality of the approach.

Hospitality can be geographically positioned, being externalised beyond the territorial state in order to minimise and contain but, crucially, to uphold the practice of hospitality. It is still present but under extreme conditions whereby hostipitality is practised. As Horst (cited in Bully 2017: 43) notes, 'the vast majority of refugees remain in the developing world and the refugee regime is now being utilised to contain refugees there'. Hospitality has been externalised in order to maintain the containment and reduction of the refugee, under the guise of humanitarian hospitality, as well as national security. From states such as Australia, Britain, the United States, as well as the EU, state sovereignty is being projected far beyond the state in order to prevent welcome, but is framed as a way to protect the refugee from undertaking hazardous journeys. The projection of hospitality is framed as in the interest of the others safety – a facade of humanitarianism is erected around the approach.

This new understanding of hospitality protects the state from the parasitical guest whilst at the same time projecting humanitarian hospitality as a facade of assistance, yet simultaneously further curtailing the practice. This is when the language of hospitality blurs from management to containment. For the state can enact hospitality, but it does not need to reside at the state level, in what Roxanne Doty (2006: 55) terms a hospitality 'not held hostage to the conceptual and legal constraints of state sovereignty and prevailing notions of national belonging'. In this regard, hospitality is set free from the confines of the state and can target the 'unknown' guests ready to claim welcome. As Dan Bulley (2017: 18) reminds us, hospitality can be a practice to keep the other where they belong, as far away from 'us as possible. Once "we" can be sure "they" won't appear at our door, we can feel both morally outraged at the evil acts of tyrants . . . and content that we are doing all we can to help.' This can be termed as humanitarian hospitality. For instance, Bulley (2017:45) speaks of humanitarian hospitality whereby refugee camps provided a level of conditional hospitality that is rather centred on providing security for the refugee guest, thus the 'space produced is different'. Yet, Bulley (2017) goes on to argue that camps 'are a product of hospitality and the interactions between hosts and guests' – be it non-state actors and the refugees, the hospitality exists within but beyond the state level – contained, managed, removed. Although providing humanitarian support, the emphasis is on exclusion, separation and maintaining that distinction – this is humanitarian hospitality.

Through the externalisation of hospitality, a state can focus on what Jonathan Darling (2009: 659) terms the 'exceptional cases', whereby a conditional humanitarian action is offered to a select minority of individuals deemed the most vulnerable and genuinely in need, thereby perpetuating further hierarchies of suffering that need to be met. The UNHCR Emergency Handbook (2018) views a humanitarian action as one principle of humanity, impartiality, neutrality – an 'altruistic, apolitical concern for human welfare' (Hehir 2010: 12). Indeed, a humanitarian action can be understood as 'explicitly attempting to legitimize . . . actions as non-partisan and moral, and hence inherently justified'. Yet the act of humanitarian hospitality is inherently strategic and does not necessarily 'complement and support states in fulfilling such responsibilities' to refugees, as the UNHCR (2018) stress it should. Through the externalisation of hospitality and the focus on exceptional cases, such as witnessed with the Syrian Vulnerable Person Resettlement Programme (VPRS)[1], a state such as Britain is able to maintain a facade of humanitarianism as well as hospitality but under such restricted, externalised practices. This facade has effectively limited, controlled and curtailed the Syrian refugees' access to hospitality, whilst excluding other non-Syrian refugees from the welcome. Only those in the geographical area of Syria are offered humanitarian hospitality, while individuals who have made the journey to Europe are deemed as unworthy of hospitality. There is a gap in the humanitarian hospitality between institutions such as the UNHCR and states like Britain, for as David Kennedy (2004: 210) argued, there is a 'sharp break between national political discretion over asylum and international institutional responsibility for refugees'. A severe practice of geographies of hierarchical hospitality is established that effectively excludes the majority of those seeking it – either at the territorial threshold of the host state, or

---

[1] A programme set up whereby Britain refused to accept refugees at her border, or as part of the EU/UNHCR quota system, but instead selected the most vulnerable from camps surrounding Syria. More discussion on the VPRS in Chapters 4 and 5.

the externalised threshold – in what can almost become a double, exclusionary practice of conditional hospitality. The refugee is not welcome at the border, but then viewed as not vulnerable enough in the camps to benefit from hospitality. Yet the state is still effectively able to wield their policy as entrenched in humanitarianism. Darling (2009: 661), drawing on Derrida, argues that 'decisions of and about hospitality should not be dismissed out of hand as exclusionary gestures, but, rather should be seen for what they are, limited, conditional, and problematic moments of sovereign distinction'. As David Kennedy (2004: 210) reminds us, 'aspiring to good, humanitarians too often mute awareness that their best ideas can have bad consequences'. Thus, an externalised practice of humanitarian hospitality is practised in order to reduce access to the state by effectively suspending hospitality at the host threshold and externalising it to the camps of the region affected whereby it is practised as a 'smokescreen for the perpetuation of repressive asylum policies of distinction, detention, deportation . . .' (Darling, 2009: 660).

Conclusion

Having explored the approach of hospitality, and then sought to develop a new externalised humanitarian hospitality, this framework of (externalised humanitarian) hospitality is pertinent for a discussion of British asylum policies and the positioning of the asylum figure. The framework of conditional hospitality allows us to understand the positioning of the asylum seeker and examine the relationships at play between the government (the host) and the refugee (the guest/ stranger).

The current approach, for example, the British position towards refuge, operates on the conditional approach to hospitality. Conditional hospitality provides the host with a level of power to wield against the guest, by dictating the terms of hospitality. In extreme cases, due to fear of abuse by the perceived 'parasite', the state will prevent the stranger from accessing hospitality in order to preserve the dignity of the institution itself. Derrida's discussion on the xenophobia of hospitality and the limitations of conditional hospitality provides a sharp reference to the darker side of what hospitality can provide, and the perceived need to protect the institution of hospitality from abuse. For conditional hospitality, as Bulley (2009: 72) notes, 'is hostile towards the other who is absolutely excluded, and hostile to the otherness that must become the same to be included'. The binarism of hospitality and hostility – what Derrida terms hostipitality – is, I argue, a defining feature of government policies and debates surrounding asylum.

In developing a perceived fear of the other, however, states such as Britain have created a practice of externalised humanitarian hospitality. This is a hospitality freed from the confines of the territorial state that is able to be projected by the state as a means to fulfil their humanitarian responsibility. Through this humanitarian hospitality, a facade of aid is developed that obscures the central practices of containment, control, deterrence that are employed. A select few can be offered welcome, thus highlighting the practice is in motion, but the welcome is founded upon a hierarchy of suffering employed by the state, with only the most vulnerable given access. The majority are deemed as parasitical, to be controlled, regulated, curtailed and primarily rejected. It is this understanding of hospitality I want to draw upon to gain a better understanding of British refugee policies, where 'to welcome the other' as Emmanuel Levinas tells us, raises questions of our freedom, our security, of our vulnerability, however justified (cited in Derrida 1999a: 29). In developing this approach of an externalised humanitarian hospitality, the next chapter introduces the politics of labelling to examine how language and labelling can be facilitated to uphold the practice of an externalised humanitarian hospitality.

CHAPTER 2

Labelling the Refugee 'Other'

The central aim of this book is to examine the role and figure of the refugee as situated in British refugee policy. It analyses the positionality of the refugee and how the politics of hospitality can be viewed as a defining feature of the British refugee system, one where fear and suspicion of the other are paramount, with hospitality defined and redefined against the refugee. This chapter analyses how hospitality towards the refugee is facilitated through the use of labelling. Within the international refugee regime, as Aristide Zolberg (cited in Ludwig 2013: 6) reminds us, there is a very 'precise' definition of a refugee that is bound in law, 'the term "refugee" has acquired a diffuse meaning in ordinary parlance'. Through what I term the politics of labelling there emerges a hierarchy that situates the label of refugee at the pinnacle, followed, in descending order, by the labels of asylum seeker, bogus asylum seeker, illegal immigrant, economic migrant, and so on. By failing to use the label of refugee, British governments have been able to successfully steer debates and create suspicion, tension and reduced sympathy towards this group within society. In 1993, Lord Jakobovits identified this practice of re-labelling refugees, during a House of Lords debate in March 1993 (HL Deb 11 March 1993, vol. 543, col. 1145). He commented, 'I cannot quite understand why the inelegant and perhaps supercilious term "asylum seeker" should have replaced the simpler word "refugee" which might evoke more sympathy.' Indeed, what Lord Jakobovits highlighted here is the politics and fracturing of language that underlies

British refugee policy. By failing to employ the label of refugee, there then emerges the possibility to frame the individual as an abusive, bogus, or failed asylum seeker, something that would not be possible with the label of refugee. You either are or are not a refugee, an individual with refugee status, or an individual seeking to attain refugee status as an international right conferred within the United Nations Convention on the Status of Refugees Article 1A.(2) (1951) and the Universal Declaration of Human Rights Article 14.(1) (1948). The label of asylum seeker or migrant, on the other hand, can fall into an array of subsequently inferior categorisations and strategies of identification that further remove the individual from the prized refugee label, thus politically destabilising and undermining the label altogether.

In engaging with the politics of labelling there are a plethora of approaches that one can adopt to examine the framing of the other as well as the politics and power relations at play. For instance, Stewart Hall's *Policing the Crisis* (1978) focuses on the term 'mugging', and how a label can do immense damage, carrying more potency than the actual activity itself by obscuring and 'demystifying' underlying causes, which can easily provide comparisons with the British asylum system. The same applies for a variety of postcolonial approaches such as Edward Said's *Orientalism* (2003) or Homi Bhabha's (1994) writing on binaries; both are extremely useful for engaging with labelling and helping to understand the politics and framing of the other. However, in examining the politics of labelling, the following section focuses on three approaches to labelling theory: that of Roger Zetter, the prominent labelling theorist within refugee studies; Howard Becker's work on deviance and labelling; and Michel Foucault's work on delinquency which covers how the delinquent is labelled, constructed, monitored and perpetuated within society. In focusing on these three approaches the chapter identifies and asserts the importance of labelling and how it is occurring for the benefit of politicians and governments to control, regulate and monitor refugee flows when offering hospitality, emphasising that labelling does not occur within a political vacuum. Labelling, as we shall discuss, is a political act since labels both include and exclude (Retzlaff 2005: 609). In examining the theories of labelling, the chapter will then turn to an analysis of the politics of labelling, focusing more on the implications of labelling, as well dissecting the labelling of the other and the exclusionary politics inherent within labelling, before concluding by turning the analysis on the often overlooked role of the labeller, and the power and distance that comes from being in that position.

Theories of Labelling: Zetter, Becker and Foucault

In engaging with theories of labelling and the refugee regime, the central theorist to begin with is Roger Zetter and his influential approach to refugees that has seen his work centred on the creation and understanding of (refugee) labels. Arguing in 1988, Zetter stressed that the label of 'refugee' 'constituted one of the most powerful labels in the repertoire of humanitarian, national, and international public policy and social differentiation', a claim that can still easily be made within the twenty-first century. Yet Zetter (1991: 60) took the approach that concealed within labels are several co-existing but contrasting identities. His approach was not necessarily focused on one model of identity being superior to another but rather focused upon three elements: 'how identities are defined and adopted; who controls them; and how the different categories complement or conflict with each other'.

In theorising labelling, Zetter (1991: 44) draws upon the process of stereotyping, which he understands as involving the

> standardization, and the formulation of clear cut categories. In the institutional setting these characteristics assume considerable power, for labelling simultaneously defines a client group and prescribes a summed set of needs (food, shelter and protection) together with appropriate distributional apparatus.

Zetter clarifies that when labels are applied, 'patterns of social and cultural norms . . . are mediated, impacted and ultimately controlled and reformulated by institutional agency'. Through the process of labelling, Zetter (1991: 40) asserts that governments have been able to categorise and create labels of identity that can be assumed, adopted and identified, with varying levels of power attributed to each label, such as 'bureaucratic procedures, resource distribution and the underlying political interests they represent, suggest that the labelling of target groups and their needs is not neutral or precise'. In this regard, Zetter (1985: 437) reflects positively that the label of refugee, 'as a policy instrument has achieved much' for it has enabled certain labelled groups access to 'networks, policies and programmes'. In this aspect, we can see that a group that has been labelled and defined has had a specific policy implemented in order to match their needs. Yet for Zetter (1985: 437), although this appears relatively unproblematic, he argues that it has 'indicated and reveals much more the nature of bureaucratic and administrative action where processes of differentiation, routines and categorizations of needs as cases are quite distinct from how the group labelled may actually perceive its own needs'. In this point, we start to witness how through policy, bureaucratisation and implementation labelling can start to be viewed as a politics in, and of, itself. For, when it comes to the labelling process, Zetter (1991: 446) reminds us that it is central to remember the role of power and who does, or does not bear power, specifically 'the non-participatory nature and powerlessness of refugees in these processes'. The politics of labelling for refugees, Zetter (1985: 446) notes, 'means conditionality, differentiation, dependency, the organization of equity'. Labelling is a process that happens to them, and not one that they are actively involved in. Although, as Foucault (1994: 341) reminds us, power is a relationship between partners, whereby there emerges a relationship of resistance. Power does not operate as completely dominate over the other but is in fact a two-way relationship whereby both parties can assert their power; it is, as Foucault notes, a 'conduct of conduct'. In this regard, power is reciprocal and, as we will see, labels can be resisted as well as self-applied.

In developing his understanding of labelling, Zetter (2007: 176) states that what has defined the current era of refuge is the distinct proliferation of new labels that are, at best, a vague interpretation, or, at worst, a relentless discriminatory term that disconnects individuals and groups from the central characteristics that equate them to being a refugee; that is, in itself, a 'stereotyped identity'. This distinct proliferation of new labels has involved an extraordinary acceleration in 're-labelling refugees and the humanitarian principles' which Zetter (2000: 353) warns has been occurring since 2000. The label of refugee has been increasingly utilised and wielded to 'marginalize, exclude, differentiate and to restrict humanitarianism'. As Zetter discussed, these new labels and stereotypes 'underpin an increasingly pervasive tendency to constrain, restrict and redefine humanitarian responses which favour the providers not the recipients' (Zetter 2000: 353). What we are witnessing is the altering of policy to suit the policy makers, the labellers, the government. What this has led to is the construction of labels such as bogus, abusive or illegal asylum seeker which have then effectively cut off and marginalised those individuals from the asylum seeker label itself, but more seriously, from the ultimate label of refugee. As such, what we have seen occurring through this politics of labelling is what Zetter terms a 'fractioning' of the original refugee label into ever smaller, inferior labels of refuge, with different categories of eligibility and entitlements bestowed on each label. Indeed, as Zetter (1991: 40) argues, this 'fractioning' of labels, far from clarifying the refugee identification process 'conveys, instead, an extremely complex set of values, and judgements which are more than just definitional'. It is within this aspect that Zetter (1991: 59) argues that labelling is so fundamentally important, as it is an inescapable part of public policy making and its language, and makes the claim that within the refugee process, 'a non-labelled way out cannot exist'. It is within this process of fractioning that new identifications and characterisations are being imposed on old identities, with the new labels, Zetter (2000: 353) argues, 'being used, not to recognize the complexity of forced migration, but more as instruments of control, restrictionism and disengagement'.

For instance, in the case of British asylum legislation, the refugee is entitled to live within Britain, work and access welfare benefits and health care; the genuine asylum seeker is entitled to remain in Britain subject to their asylum application; they are not, however, entitled to work or to access mainstream benefits but instead receive 'asylum support' and can apply for accommodation through the Home Office's dispersal policy (Gower 2015). In contrast, the individual labelled as a bogus asylum seeker is likely to be detained then deported. During this process they will then we re-labelled as a failed asylum seeker – someone fraudulently seeking to enter Britain by abusing the refugee system (Gibney 2008). The (perceived illegal) economic migrant will be denied entry, and if found, detained and deported. Accordingly, when examining the British fragmentation of the refugee label into sub-categories of genuine/bogus asylum seekers, it is easy to see how the process of labelling has allowed for political assumptions surrounding refugee identity to become immersed in 'ostensibly neutral bureaucratic categories, such as "refugee"' (Zetter 2007: 185).

The emergence of highly politicised labels such as bogus and illegal, particularly in response to rising asylum numbers of the late 1990s and early 2000s in Britain, as well as growing criticism of the states' perceived inadequate responses to quell the 'flow' (Boswell et al. 2015), has resulted in the label of refugee itself being removed from its traditional roots in the United Nations Convention and Protocol Relating to the Status of Refugees (1951) and becoming a 'highly privileged prize' for which only a small minority are deemed to be eligible. Zetter (2007: 182) argues that the 'proliferation of labels . . . underpins a deliberately transformative process to create far less-preferential categories'. As Zetter elaborates, the use of labels like refugee can actually appear as a 'benign' or even a kind way in which to reach as many 'potential beneficiaries' as possible. The label in this instance can appear as all-inclusive. Yet, Zetter (1991: 51) warns that the act of being labelled a refugee can

> come to mean a number of things over time . . . labels assume a much more powerful significance. They serve as a linguistic shorthand for policies, programmes and bureaucratic requirements – practices which are instrumental in categorizing and differentiating between facets of an identity.

The result, for Zetter, is that the label of refugee becomes further removed from the lived experience of those facing forced displacement. The result is a myriad of new labels, categorisations and statuses, grounded in hostile politics, that Zetter (2000: 351) affirms are established in order to effectively 'exclude or marginalize large numbers of forced migrants to deny the basic premise of protection embodied in the [Refugee] convention'. The ultimate outcome for a state's refugee regime is a 'compromised humanitarianism', whereby state policy trumps humanitarian practices in effectively overriding the international refugee regime (Zetter 2000: 353).

When examining the use of labelling, we can also draw upon Howard Becker's theory of labelling. In his 1966 work *Outsiders*, Becker focused on the process of labelling and how individuals labelled are constructed, identified and labelled by the majority group within a society. Becker (1991: 9) argues that within a society, social groups create rules and attempt to have those rules enforced where necessary. In developing his argument, Becker focuses on the example of deviant behaviour. In discussing deviance, he notes that it is not the behaviour itself that is deviant, but rather that it has been labelled deviant by other social groups who have enforced rules regarding that behaviour. In a way, certain behaviours come to be understood as deviant – they are learned to be deviant, rather than inherently being deviant. Those who are said to have broken the rules of society are framed as deviants: the outsiders of society. As Becker (1991: 162) explains:

> [deviance] . . . in the sense I have been using it, of publicly labelled wrongdoing – is always the result of enterprise. Before any act can be viewed as deviant, and before any class can be labelled and treated as outsiders for committing the act, someone must have made the rule which defined the act as deviant.

In a sense, it is the majority social group dictating what behaviours are socially acceptable behavioural patterns within society. The labelled are positioned outside the normal social structure, with some social groups far more susceptible to being labelled deviant and with the rules tending 'to be applied more too some persons than others' (Becker 1991: 12). Becker (1991: 161) goes on to stress that when it comes to the process of deviance,

> We must see deviance, and the outsiders who personify the abstract conception as a consequence of a process of interaction between people, some of whom in the service of their own interests make and enforce rules which catch others who, in the service of their own interests, have committed acts which are labelled deviant.

Similar to the deviance label, the label of refugee or asylum seeker exposes an individual to a plethora of negative connotations that marginalise their situation, as well as positioning them as a threat that needs to be dealt with. Asylum has been heavily politicised since the 1990s, with government responses emphasising the heavy handedness apparently needed to address the perceived problem, and the rhetoric of 'floods', 'swamps' and 'tides' being increasingly drawn upon to highlight the threat and security risk presented by refugees or asylum seekers. The label asylum seeker or others, such as bogus, illegal, clandestine, abusive or economic migrant, are all socially and politically constructed and have emerged from parliamentary debates into legislation and regulations, as will be explored in Chapter 3.

Since 1990, consecutive British governments have decided that certain behaviours from would-be refugees would no longer be deemed acceptable, for instance, arriving without passports, without visas or via a deemed 'safe' third country (McFadyen 2016). As such, those asylum seekers who are not able to comply with the set government criteria are labelled with the connotation that they are merely seeking economic benefits rather than genuinely seeking sanctuary (Crawley 2010; Gibney 2004: 122; McFadyen 2016). The label is applied uniformly, obscuring the individual cases that it is meant to apply to – what Zetter spoke of as the loss of the humanitarian element within state refugee protection. However, as Becker (1991: 9) warns us, 'the process of labelling may not be infallible'. There may be individuals who end up being labelled deviant or bogus, illegal or abusive asylum seekers who have in fact not broken any rules. Conversely, there may be people labelled as refugees or asylum seekers who actually are not. In the end, the government, the Home Office and the Border Agencies who engage with the asylum applications view the label first, rather than the individual stories behind the label. The label of asylum seeker, rather than refugee, becomes the 'master status' whereby this 'identification proves to be more important than most others', with the individual being labelled as an asylum seeker first, before other identifications are made (Becker 1991: 33). As noted, you either are, or are not a refugee, whereas the label of asylum seeker has been allowed to become a rather ambiguous label, removing the individual from the prized refugee label, and instead into an array of inferior labels.

Labelling is a conscious decision by one group to label another – shaping and normalising behaviours, whilst establishing distinctions between individuals, normally to the detriment of the labelled. It is a bureaucratic process that enables the government to mystify issues such as refuge, with the end result being that the label resonates more with society and instils fear, far more than the real facts of the matter would have done.

Becker is not alone in his discussion of the labelling effect on delinquents within society. The prominent critical theorist Michel Foucault writes of the process of labelling in reference to the delinquent in *Discipline and Punish* ([1975] 1991), tracing the emergence of deviant behaviour in the French prison system. He argues that the prison system fabricated the existence of the delinquent, through the use of 'violent constraints' imposed upon the individual. The prison, for Foucault (1991: 266), is meant to offer a place of correction, education and rehabilitation but instead functions 'in the form of an abuse of power'. Although viewed as a failing of the system, the emergence of the delinquent is actually its greatest product. For the *raison d'être* of the prison is not 'to think of man in society, it is to create an unnatural, useless and dangerous existence' (Foucault 1991: 266). Foucault affirmed that through the processes and power of the prison system, certain types of behaviours and illegalities are isolated and actually formed within the system, such as delinquency. He noted (1991: 277)

> One should not see in delinquency the most intense, most harmful form of illegality, the form that the penal apparatus must try to eliminate through imprisonment because of the danger it represents; it is rather an effect of penality . . . that makes it possible to differentiate, accommodate and supervise illegalities.

Foucault (1991: 272) raised the question of what is achieved through the apparent 'failure' of the prison system. The system allows for the continuation of delinquency, the emergence of the 'habitual offender' and for a fraternity of delinquents to accumulate that are quite distinct from more hardened forms of criminals.

However, for Foucault, it is not just the constraints and abuses experienced within the prison system that are at issue here in creating and maintaining the delinquent. Rather, it is the continuation of the surveillance culture and monitoring of behaviour once the individual has been freed from the system and is within the wider community that reproduces the delinquent behaviour. As Foucault (1991: 256) wrote:

> The conditions to which the free inmates are subjected necessarily condemn them to recidivism: they are under the surveillance of the police; they are assigned to a particular residence, or forbidden others; they leave prison with a passport that they must show everywhere they go and which mentions the sentence that they have served. Being on the loose, being unable to find work, leading the life of vagabonds are the most frequent factors in recidivism.

This approach to delinquents has echoes of Zetter's discussion on the positivity of labelling – a group has been labelled and defined and has had a specific policy implemented in order to match their (assumed) needs. Even on leaving the confines of the prison, the individual is denied full entry into the ranks of the citizenry. The individual is then forced to adopt a marginalised position within society with rights such as liberty, employment and freedom denied. Through their position within the community and the surveillance imposed upon them, the individual is branded. As Foucault (1994) argues, knowledge is circulated throughout society by the dominant discourses and knowledge of the time, thereby reproducing power against the delinquent.

This forces the individual into certain behaviours in order to survive, behaviours that feed back, not into hardened crime, but delinquency, thus perpetuating the prison system cycle. In this regard the prison system and the branding that follows release are

> not intended to eliminate offences, but rather to distinguish them, to distribute them, to us them; that it is not so much that they render docile those who are liable to transgress the law, but that they tend to assimilate the transgression of the laws in a general tactics of subjection. (Foucault 1991: 272)

Indeed, Foucault (2009: 19), speaking in his Prison Lecture of 1976, argues that the prison system 'condemns those it has recruited to a life of crime because of the effects of social alienation and the criminal record'. As William Connolly (1983: 332) observed:

> It is well known that modern prisons breed hardened criminals. That effect, Foucault insists, is not one of its failures but the sign of its greatest success. Modern penality depoliticizes crime; it draws attention to the character of the criminal and away from the power of the regime; and it separates the criminal from other disaffected elements of the population.

However, through a reading of Foucault (1991: 272), he highlights that the delinquent is separated from the hardened criminal, with a distinction being made between them in the eyes of the law – with delinquent behaviour being accepted, encouraged and viewed as non-political or non-economic in nature. It is here especially that through Foucault's understanding of the delinquent, and how they are labelled, constructed, monitored and perpetuated within society, that we can draw comparisons with the figure of the refugee. The delinquent is presented as separate from the (criminal) population – an abnormality, or what Foucault (1991: 286) terms a 'strangeness' from the lower classes of society – and is presented as 'close by, everywhere present and everywhere to be feared'. The delinquent, just as the refugee, is presented and labelled as 'very close and quite alien, a perpetual threat to everyday life, but extremely distant in its origin and motives, both everyday and exotic in the milieu in which it takes place' (Foucault 1991: 286). In this regard, the delinquent is also relegated as other within society, residing at the margins of society. Much like the refugee, the delinquent is consumed by the label, with the individuality of their behaviour and actions being lost within the wider societal label of delinquent. As Zetter noted, a group has successfully been labelled and defined and has had a specific policy implemented in order to match their needs. Forced to the margins of society, the delinquent, like the refugee, becomes an object of fear in society.

Through the work of Zetter, Becker and Foucault, this chapter has sought to highlight the significance as well as the power of labelling, both on the labelled and the labeller. By labelling an individual or a group, the labeller is socially demarcating a specific group within society and, in the instance of the refugee, removing them from the normal spheres of social engagement (such as employment, benefits, housing, health care). Labelling is a conscious decision by one group to frame another, shaping and normalising behaviours whilst establishing distinctions between individuals, normally to the detriment of the labelled. It is a bureaucratic process, that enables governments to mystify issues such as refuge, with the end result being that the label resonates more with society and instils fear to a greater degree than the real fact of the matter would have done. For it has come to be expected, as Helton (2003: 13–16) warned, that

> The arrival of uninvited people in need can also exacerbate fears of difference and cultural confrontations, a point not lost on politicians in democratic countries. The terrible evil which produces refugees can be insulated from remedy by an indifference that arises from personal insecurity . . . the common thread then, is fear: fear that gives rise to refuge flight, fear that keeps people from offering haven to those in need. The combinations and permutations of insecurity that emerge in particular situations shape fundamentally the policy response, whether generous or grudging.

Labelling is political by nature and through the use of labels, the government has been able to set and define the agenda regarding asylum. Through the continuous use of the term asylum seeker, and then the introduction of terms such as bogus, the government has been able to successfully fracture the label of refugee. Refugees are no longer here to seek refuge, but asylum, and in doing so many will be found to be bogus. Through the process of labelling, the system of refuge is fractured, providing the government with the opportunity to point to growing abuse of the asylum system and protect the borders from the apparent hordes of refugees intent on abusing the welfare system. Labelling in this regard has provided the government with the power to redefine the notion of asylum and refuge within Britain.

The Politics of Labelling

Now, this might seem like a pedantic argument, squabbling over the use of the terms migrant or refugee, but words matter, labels matter, and how we label someone impacts not only on their position but also on our interactions and responsibilities towards them. For labelling does not occur within a political vacuum, and this really needs to be remembered: the creation and application of labels is always political. Labelling is a conscious decision by one group to label another – shaping and normalising behaviours whilst establishing distinctions between individuals, normally to the detriment of the labelled, as noted above. As Geof Wood (1985: 352) asserts, 'it is a relationship of power, asymmetrical and one-sided'. At the heart of labelling is the use of power, and how label-ling needs to be understood as an 'instrument of power', as Aristide Zolberg (Zolberg et al. 1989: 274) refers to it. Arguing about labels may appear pedantic, but labelling can shift or sustain power rela-tions in ways that trigger social dislocation and prejudice efforts to achieve greater equity within society (Moncrieffe 2007: 1). It is important to remember that the label of the refugee is socially con-structed, bearing and representing certain 'complex legal, ethical and political connotations' (Vigil and Abidi 2018: 54).

In examining the politics of labelling further, Stuart Hall (1978: 19) observed that 'labels are important, especially when applied to dramatic public events. They not only place and identify those events; they assign events to a context.' In the instance of refugees, Hall would argue that the term has carried more potency than the action itself; or more seriously, that the term eventually became disengaged and removed from its societal roots and origins. In this respect, society comes to understand merely the label of refugee, rather than the wider societal implications as to why it is happen-ing, or the grounded legal, humanitarian frameworks of its origins. Similarly to Hall, Zolberg (Zolberg et al. 1989: 274) also affirms that in regards to refugee policy, 'language serves to mystify rather than clarify', arguing that 'greater awareness of linguistic mystifi-cation is the basis for an informed public debate and a rational refugee policy'. For the label becomes associated with issues or problems surrounding socio-economic concerns that actually are not reflected in the realities of the livid experience of those seeking refuge. Georgia Cole (2017: 9) through her research highlighted that this mystification of the label allows states and institutions to avoid their legal and financial responsibility to the refugees. The label of refugee provides a distortion in reality, or what Tazreena Sjjad (2018) refers to as a transformation of reality, that supports repressive government asylum policies as well as highlighting the potency of labelling.

By altering, transforming and demystifying the lived reality of the refugee experience, the politics of labelling is able to determine who is genuine and in need of refugee protection within states such as Britain as well as who should be excluded, by offering the pretence of 'value-neutral' categorisations, obscuring the fact that they are products of bureaucratic processes. This process of labelling, as Edward Horesh (1985) discusses, represents 'relations of power between the strong and the weak' but importantly, represents power not in a 'naked' form, but power that is 'dressed and labelled, or appears more palatable'. The labelling or framing of such politics accounts for what Murray Edelman (cited in Mulvey 2010: 445) refers to as the mass public response 'to currently conspicuous political symbols: not to "facts" and not to moral codes embedded in the character or soul, but to gestures and speeches that make up the drama of the state'. It distorts and demystifies reality and for Edward Horesh (1985: 513), it 'constrains our minds and inhibits lateral thinking', but in doing so, it perpetually reinforces the difference in power relations between the labelled and the labeller. As such, as Jaideep Gupte and Lyla Mehta (2007: 65) stress, 'there is a disjuncture between how forced migrants view themselves and how current policy frameworks view them', thus reaffirming the strategy of identification employed within the politics of labelling.

In this sense then, the politics of labelling can be understood as a bureaucratic process, as Zetter referred to it, that enables a government to mystify issues such as refuge, with the end result being that the label resonates more with society and instils far more fear than the real facts would do. Thereby, Wood (1985: 353) argues, the politics of labelling 'reveals more about the process of authoritative designation, agenda-setting and so on than about the characteristics of the labelled . . . labels misrepresent or more deliberately falsify the situation and role of the labelled'. Wood (1985: 352) acknowledges that

> labelling is the attribute of a certain kind of public management of resources – namely bureaucratic, professional, formal, institutionalised and often central. It is the counterpart of access in that the authors of labels, of designations, have determined the rules of access to particular resources and privileges. They are settling the rules of inclusion and exclusion . . .

What we have been witnessing, particularly within the British asylum system, has been a fracturing of the label of refugee into 'inferior sub-categories', further removing the asylum seeker from the status of refugee (McFadyen 2016). This has resulted in new labels seeping into the process of asylum, and circumventing the original refugee label, with asylum seeker, economic migrant, failed asylum seeker dominating the refugee policy language. This has resulted in what David Turton (cited in Silvereira 2015: 4) terms a 'hierarchy of suffering' emerging where the refugee label becomes a 'prized status and expensive commodity' in and of itself.

Labelling, the Other and Resistance

As we discussed, labelling can be understood as a politics. A political bureaucratic process in itself that fracture labels and identities, distorting reality in order to maintain power over the labelled. Through this process of fracturing the label, new labels emerge that are established from the fracture, but they ultimately only 'impoverish' the original label by marginalising the original meaning and form. Yet it is important to remember that, regardless of the process of fracturing, the original label of refugee is not destroyed but rather is hidden, removed, distorted. As Georgia Cole (2017: 7) argues, 'the legal bedrock of the label . . . provides a convenient resource for humanitarian actors to 'hide' behind when establishing an ethical, political and financial bottom line to their activities'. The politics of refugee labelling has allowed the British state, for example, to strengthen its opposition to asylum and seek to increase deportations whilst at the same time, 'being globally accepted as a human rights champion' (Sjjad 2018: 40). Indeed, through the politics of labelling there is a natural establishment of binarisms of '"us" versus "them", or even "them" versus "another them"' (Gupte and Mehta 2007: 69). Labelling naturally establishes an other. Reece Jones (2016: 167), writing in *Violent Borders*, examined the binarisms that emerged within the refugee experience, and the centrality of borders, the state and citizenship to the binarism. He wrote,

> The distinction between outside and inside, between native and foreigner, pervades the political discourse in countries around the world because it is part of the foundation of the state as an institution. The place-based version of humanity plays a powerful role in the contemporary public discourse in many countries, as migrations are represented as a threat to the economic, cultural and political system of the state.

Jones asserted that the exclusion of the external group from state resources and opportunity is founded upon the assumption that the 'in-group should be protected no matter what, with little regard for the effect it might have on the other and without questioning why there is a distinction between "us" and "them" in the first place'. This is what Hannah Arendt (2003: 296) referred to as the fallacy of the 'right to have rights' and the assumed universality of human rights. The right to basis security can only be guaranteed through citizenship, as such 'the Rights of Man, supposedly inalienable, proved to be unenforceable'. For who is going to uphold the rights of the non-citizen other?

This shaping of the refugee migrant other is done through the use of the politics of labelling and the categorisation of the other as a threat. This establishment of the other as a threat can be viewed similarly to Edward Said's (2003: 3) Orientalism – 'the Western style for dominating, restructuring and having authority over the Orient'. The construction and wielding of the oriental other is, as Said (2003) stressed, an unequal relationship of power, of domination of varying degrees of complex hegemon, between the Occident and the Orient. Indeed, this unequal relationship of 'us' versus 'them', Jones (2016: 169) argues, can be understood through the politics of language for 'they are not fundamental truths that are universal: they are a set of agreements within a particular society that establish a set of rules to decide what is true, but it does not have to be that way'. It is established political power over the refugee other. Zolberg (1989: 4) argues that defining refugees as other for the purpose of policy implementations requires a political choice and an ethical judgement. In being labelled a refugee, there is a process of 'conformity [where] circumstances of "story" had to be relinquished to the bureaucratic dictates of "case"'(Zetter 1991: 47). This has resulted in the label of the refugee being one of the most powerful labels within the repertoire of humanitarian practice. As Zetter (1991: 39) argues, 'from the first procedures of status determination – who is a refugee? – to the structural determinants of life changes which this identity then engenders, labels infuse the world of refugees'. Specific labels guarantee, to reiterate Arendt's (2003: 278) point, 'the right to have rights'. Yet, through the politics of labelling and political dominance, the refugee is denied the right to have rights through the process of othering.

Margaret Somers (cited in Ludwig 2013: 13) argues that 'continuing to label individuals as refugees is synonymous with a process of othering, and therefore, undermines potential membership in a new society'. For labelling, as Zetter (1991: 51) stresses, provides an 'identity in one conceptual language, refugees in all these cases have had imposed on them a radically different language. Whether deliberately or in ignorance, this imposition dominates the behaviour of refugee societies.' For instance, being labelled as 'passive victims in need of rescue and help' undermines the resilience and strength of refugees, placing a further burden upon refugees that is then perpetuated further by the host society viewing them as 'socially and economically dependent' that only further hinders their integration (Ludwig, 2013: 13). As Barbra Harrell-Bond (cited in Ludwig 2013: 12) stressed, labels such as 'refugee' reinforced the idea of refugees as 'submissive and helpless . . . who are waiting for something to happen'. Yanery Vigil and Catherine Abidi (2018: 53) speak of the refugee label as bearing 'assumptions of vulnerability and lack of recognition of the multiple identities and labels embraced by and embodied on refugees'. The refusal to accept or 'wear' an imposed label can be viewed as a form of resistance against the dominant – labeller – host society. For as Vivienne Jabri (2013: 31) reminds us, the 'postcolonial subject carries a legacy of resistance against foreign domination'.

Indeed, within literature such as Ludwig (2013) or Gupte and Mehta (2007) the label of refugee is viewed as a 'stigma' that denies refugees their agency; or, as Ludwig (2013: 14) argues, the label of refugee can be perceived as an 'eternal label and identity' or what Zetter (1998: 1) terms 'institutionalised dependency'. It is specifically through the process of resisting labels that language and 'the power of attaching labels to identify especially is very much an ongoing political issue' (Retzlaff 2005: 620). This is when the potency of labelling becomes extremely apparent.

Certainly, the act of being labelled can render the refugee an object and can be viewed as a silencing of the individual's agency. Sara McKinnon (2008) refers to this as the 'objectification of refugees' – they are no longer subject, but rather othered objects 'in need of assistance, training and a host of other resettlement services, though never to speak and act of their own accord in the public'. Much like Edward Said's (2003: 3) Orientalism, labelling is a way for the West to dominate, restructure and maintain authority over the other with rhetoric founded on the distinction between East and West, in what Said (2003: 7) terms 'a collective notion identifying "us" Europeans as against all "those" non-Europeans' founded on the 'European superiority over Oriental backwardness'. Labelling, as Geof Wood (1985: 364) discusses, is a process with the central purpose of 'disorganzing the dominated, the weak, the vulnerable, the poor or just the excluded'. For it is important to highlight, as Tazreena Sjjad's (2018: 56) stresses, that despite the vast array of labels that have emerged through the fractured refugee label

refugees, displaced, migrants, asylum seekers, expelled, stateless, repatriated, returned, illegal, unauthorised, undocumented, irregular – [they] have not indicated a broadening of the humanitarian safety-net to recognise drivers of displacement, but have, rather, reinforced the power of the state to create systems of hierarchy, making hyper-visible those who have transgressed a range of boundaries, and violated the natural order of the state-citizen relationship.

It is at this point that once again we need to reinforce the real world implications that labelling or representations of certain groups can have within society. As Hall (cited in Ratzlaff 2005: 620) reminds us, the labelling applied to certain groups within society, such as refugees, has 'real world consequences with respect to the lives, rights and positions of the so presented group in society'. A stark example of this was right-wing Hungarian Prime Minister Victor Orban (cited in Al Jazeera 2015b), who stated in October 2015, during the height of the European Refugee Crisis, that Hungary was closing its southern border, erecting a steel fence the length of the border. Orban argued that he was 'duty-bound to secure the borders of the European Union to protect what he calls the prosperity, security and "Christian values" of Europe'. Or most recently, in December 2018, British Home Secretary Sajid Javid referred to those attempting to cross the English Channel as 'illegal migrants' even though the individuals were seeking asylum. Indeed, through this example, the objectification of refugees, as well as the fracturing and transformation of labels is at play, with those seeking refuge 'seen as objects either requiring help or posing a threat, not as subjects with agency and voice' (Vigil and Abidi 2018, 55). By fracturing the labelling, denying the use of refugee at the discretion of Home Office authorities, those labelled as 'illegal migrants' are othered and positioned with no rights at all, even denied the international right to refuge (Elgot and Walker 2019), in what Zolberg (1989: 274) argues is the 'instrumental use of language to legitimize differential treatment' for specific client populations.

The Power of the Labeller

In order to conclude the discussion on labelling, the final section will turn to an analysis of those conducting the labelling, that is, the labeller. The labeller is an often overlooked protected group within the research of labelling, where the onus is mainly on the politics and implications for the labelled group. Often the labeller escapes attention. Here I am following the advice of David Smith (1995: 86), who stresses 'rather than focusing on the labelled, focus on who is doing the labelling, analyse their power to label and define'. For as Sherene Razack (2008: 88) reminds us, it is important to pay attention to the 'describers and imaginers whose gaze constructs asylum seekers from the third world'.

For labelling, as Joy Moncrieffe (2007: 11) reminds us, 'is pervasive and inevitable' to the extent that she highlights that we 'all label and are, in turn, all labelled'. Moncrieffe argues that 'labelling regulates social interaction: it helps us to define the terms on which we relate to "others"; without it, interaction would be chaotic and inefficient'. It is, as Geof Wood (1985: 347) asserts, the 'act of politics involving conflict as well as authority'. Indeed, the discussion now is not on whether we label, 'but which, by whom, under what conditions, for what purpose, with what effects!' (Wood 1985: 353). These are the questions that need to be addressed in order to fully grapple with the politic of labelling, and the power to label.

Grahl-Madsen identified in 1983 that 'part of the tragedy of our times [was] that several states by various methods are seeking to prevent or at least to discourage refugees from reaching their shores to seek sanctuary' (cited in Costello and Mouzourakis 2016: 57). Over thirty years later, his warning still rings true. By employing the politics of labelling, states such as Britain have been able to circumvent their international responsibility, by reframing, fracturing and demystifying the refugee other. As will be discussed in Chapter 4, rather than a European Refugee Crisis, it is presented as a European Migrant crisis – this is an overt tactic of deflection and labelling that operates in the British state's interests. Through labelling, the crisis can be trivialised, normalised and deflected. As Luc Boltanski (1999: 17) argues, a person 'who does nothing and fails to act is not only "casually" responsible for an evil he could have prevented . . . but he does nothing because he has an interest in averting his gaze'. The labeller, through the process of labelling and fracturing, operates the politics of labelling as a means to demystify the crisis, averting the humanitarian gaze.

Importantly though, when it comes to the labeller, labelling usually occurs from 'a distance, with little to no contact between the labeller and the labelled'. The geographical distance, Moncrieffe (2007: 11) argues, facilitates a reduction in responsibility and accountability to the other for how they are labelled but also the implications of said label. This 'hegemonic framing and labelling', obscures diversity and difference, with the intended successful outcome being the creating of a narrow, singular response whilst marginalising salient issues. Indeed, Moncrieffe (2006: 38) argues that due to the distance, as well as the base, fixed assumptions developed of the distant other, the labeller may 'fail to recognise the challenges that encounter may bring'. The power of labelling, or the power of the labeller, has been equated to Jeremy Bentham's panopticon, 'which contorts power relations to allow seeing without ever been seen' (Gupte and Mehta 2007: 67).The architectural structure of the panopticon induces in those being observed 'a state of conscious and permanent visibility that assures the automatic functioning of power'. And regardless of whatever field it is put to use in, be it prisons or refugee policy, 'homogenous effects of power' are produced (Foucault 1991: 202).

The labeller can see the other, hold power over the other, (re) positioning the other without needing to interact with the other. The power of the labeller, and the distance between the labeller and the labelled, links back to the previous discussion on the loss of reality and the demystification of the other, resulting in a reality gap between refugees and policy makers. The distance further demystifies the lived experience of the refugee.

And this argument works well in relation to the British government and the European Union, who insist on still utilising the label of 'illegal migration', with its inherent implications of secrecy, deviance and criminality, and as the harbinger of security risks (Sjjad 2018: 55). As Luc Boltanski (1999: 11–13) asserts, 'to arouse pity, suffering and wretched bodies must be conveyed in such a way as to affect the sensibility of those more fortunate'. However, when the other is being labelled as a migrant, undeserving of our sympathy and sanctuary, the outcome is not one of immediate help or assistance. Our pity of the other, as Boltanski (1999) addresses, operates from a 'standpoint of distance', as the other need not be in our presence. But 'when the other comes together in person to invade the space of those more fortunate than they and with the desire to mix with them, to live in the same places and to share the same objects, then they no longer appear as unfortunates' (Boltanksi 1999: 13). As Arendt (2003) says, they are transformed into 'les enragés'.

Concerning the refugee crisis, what we are witnessing is how 'negative labels (and implications) can disempower groups through the creation of potent negative stereotypes and how this can be a powerful means of exercising social control and a tool to manipulate identities'. Indeed, within the refugee crisis was the power of social media to champion the refugee, offering solidarity and support, specifically through the use of hashtags such as #refugeewelcome or #SolidaritywithRefugees. But, the problem with labels such as this, even in solidarity and welcome to the refugee, is that they rely 'on the assumption that other migrants who do not fit the limited definition of a refugee are not welcome' (Retzlaff 2005: 610). This will be an argument that I will develop further within Chapter 4 on Labelling and the Mediterranean Crisis. For labels, as we have been arguing, 'carry with them emotional effect and stereotypes, which in turn can mould impressions and sway public opinion' (Merolla et al. 2013: 793). This is the power of the labeller.

Conclusion

The distinction between inside and outside, between native and foreign, pervades the political discourse in countries around the world because it is part of the foundation of the state as an institution – the state as the sovereign actor. Society operates through the practice of inclusion and exclusion, be it citizens, refugees, asylum seekers or stateless people. Society is structured in a way to respond to each one, or to marginalise and exclude others. To decide the right to life and the right to die, viewing the non-citizen other as a societal disease that needs to be eradicated (Marino 2016). In reflecting back to Derrida, he argued that the label and the experience of the refugee in this century have 'undergone a mutation . . . The words "refugee," "exile," "deported," "displaced person" and even "foreigner" have changed their meaning' (Derrida 2000). But, rather than a mutation, I argue that what we are witnessing is a politics of labelling. The language and vocabulary that surrounds the figure of the asylum seeker does vary in its range but is 'singular in its intention – to convey an image of marginality, dishonesty, a threat, unwelcomed . . .' (Zetter 2007: 184). Through the politics of labelling we are able to witness the fear and suspicion of the other that emerges through conditional hospitality, and how the fear of the abusive other leads to the state establishing multiple labels of inferiority in order to protect the right to refuge from being abused. The politics of labelling allows (multiple) British governments to determine the level of hospitality towards the individual in question. The genuine asylum seeker will be welcomed, but conditional hospitality will generally reign. With the fracturing of the refugee label, individuals will be increasingly unable to attain the label refugee and will fall into inferior categorisations, thus incurring hostility from the state.

The MP Alistair Darling (1991), in a parliamentary debate in 1991, highlighted the emergence of various other labels within refugee policy, particularly the fractured labels emerging at that time such as bogus refugees. He questioned, 'what is a bogus refugee? Is it someone who has applied and been rejected? That is an important point, because the Government seem to suggest that, by definition, if one does not receive asylum, one must be bogus'. And it is this that makes the notion of labelling so powerful. Through the politics of labelling, the government has created an idealised notion of what constitutes a genuine asylum seeker through British asylum policies. In doing so, it has set limitations and restrictions upon asylum, a process that is already fairly constrained. By adding additional restrictions to refuge, such as travel restrictions, British governments have managed to control the field of asylum and narrow the target audience. Thus hospitality is positioned firmly within the realm of conditional hospitality, with the government functioning through the framework of hostipitality. The construction of a hierarchy of refugee labels is testament to the fear of the abusive stranger who is intent on exploiting the hospitality of the host state. Portrayed as merely economic migrants, asylum seekers are seen to have abused the hostipitality of the refugee system for their own needs and subsequently are blamed for creating backlogs and queues and wasting the resources of the state.

Having examined the politics of hospitality and the language of labelling, the next three chapters are case studies to highlight how the politics of hospitality, facilitated by the politics of labelling, has determined the position of the refugee within British refugee policy. They examines first, the internal refugee practices and the construction of an idealised genuine refugee, then second, British externalised hospitality within the Mediterranean crisis, where hospitality is projected beyond the confines of the state, at the same time as refugees are re-labelled when they move geographically – losing the refugee label the closer they get to Britain. The refugee figure, bound by the politics of labelling, operates through the framework of hospitality, allowing the British state to retain their humanitarian credentials, but under their own restricted terms and conditions. The third case study then offers a counter-narrative approach, by examining local and community practices of hospitality in response to the Mediterranean crisis.

CHAPTER 3

The British Hostile Environment and the Creation of a Genuine Refugee

[T]here is a genuine problem with asylum in this country . . . The proper way forward is to do what we are doing: introducing tough new asylum measures that will allow genuine asylum seekers through, but will halt those bogus asylum seekers who do nothing but harm to the cause of proper asylum seekers. (Blair HC Deb 2 February 2000: vol. 343 col 1048–103)

What is a bogus refugee? Is it someone who has applied and been rejected? . . . the Government seem to suggest that, by definition, if one does not receive asylum, one must be bogus. I should have thought that a bogus refugee or a bogus asylum seeker is someone who knew all along that he had no chance and that his application was ill-founded. (Darling HC Deb 13 November 1991: vol. 198, col 1082)

The figure of the refugee in Britain has occupied a precarious position over the last 100 years. Governments have been open to providing hospitality to the refugee – an individual who can apply for asylum 'owing to a well-founded fear of being persecuted for reasons of race, religion, nationality, membership of a particular social group or political opinion' (UNHCR 1951). Indeed, the consecutive governments have been at pains to proclaim Britain's longstanding humanitarian record in relation to refugees (Stevens 1998b: 9). Yet, since 1990, when annual refugee applications spiked at 26,205 (Hawkins 2014), consecutive British governments have been caught between positioning the refugee as a humanitarian figure in need of refuge, in what has been termed a 'paradoxical response' (Gibney 2014).

Through consecutive British governments, an idealised categorisation of the would-be refugee has emerged. The resulting product has been the emergence of a tangible one-size-fits-all figure of a genuine refugee. This figure has been upheld as honourable, legal and legitimate. Governments since the 1990s have presented the genuine refugee as the pinnacle of refuge: they will have particular experiences, adhere to certain modes of travel and be knowledgeable of the national asylum rules. This figure is upheld as the true refugee. Anyone unable to meet these criteria of the genuine refugee are labelled as bogus, as failed asylum seekers or more commonly now, as economic migrants. Indeed, through the creation and proliferation of labels, governments have been able to 'engage in an act of power' (Barnett and Finnemore 1999: 711) against the refugee, with the group reduced simply to what Guy Goodwin-Gill (cited in Behrman, 2018: 1) refers to as a 'unit of displacement' whereby refugees are required to be categorised, controlled and warehoused, preferably outside Britain.

The main objective of this chapter is to examine how consecutive British governments have sought to fracture the label of refugee. It focuses on the four governments since 1990: the Conservative government from 1990 to 1997; New Labour (1997–2010); the Conservative and Liberal Democrat coalition government (2010–15); and the Conservative government (2015 – present). Although addressing specific governments, it argues that each of these governments has followed the same line of logic regarding asylum, adopting similar non-partisan approaches and rhetoric towards the refugee; regardless of Conservative or New Labour governance, the hostile approach to refugees has been the same.

The chapter addresses how the politics of hospitality and labelling operate in the state's interest and at the expense of the refugee. The core argument identifies five ways in which these four governments have sought to establish the label of a genuine asylum seeker. The chapter also draws on the case study of the Windrush generation and the British intensification of hostile environment policies that occurred under the premiership of Cameron and May from 2010 onwards, in order to highlight how government labels, categories and policy alter and change, resulting in a hospitable group facing open hostility from the host state.

In doing so, following Derrida, this chapter identifies the government as the host, who has the power to offer hospitality to the guest, the refugee, and highlights how this fragile relationship can be altered significantly in order to suit the needs of the host state.

Drawing upon the language and framing of the refugee from parliamentary archives, the chapter presents a narrative of an idealised refugee figure that has been constructed through consecutive governments, at the expense of the refugee. In doing so, it argues that what we are witnessing within the British asylum system is the politics of hospitality, whereby hostility is the overriding reaction to the refugee. Indeed, what this chapter is discussing is the establishment and development of the hostile environment, of hostipitality, a series of policies, legislation and practices that have been implemented by successive governments, regardless of political leanings in order to control, reduce and fragment refugee (and immigration) numbers within the country.

Yasmin Ibrahim and Anita Howarth (2018b: 370) argue that in Britain there has been a 'distinctive . . . tradition of humanitarian refugee from the nineteenth century, a period of open borders that coincided with a new secular morality centred on the human in relation to the state to the unapologetically hostile environment'. This chapter documents the construction of the hostile environment within the British asylum system, which can be viewed as a 'virtually uninterrupted message of hostility and rejection', in what Matthew Gibney (2014: 164) refers to as 'schizophrenic response' where the British state has sought to 'embrace asylum but spurn the asylum seeker'.

Constructing the Genuine Refugee

The following discussions are an examination of the idealised genuine refugee that has been constructed through the practice of hospitality and the politics of labelling – identifying and categorising behaviours that a genuine refugee should be expected to hold. The categorisations of genuineness operate within the British refugee system and the vast majority of refugees are caught between the labels of genuine versus bogus (or more commonly now, failed, illegal, or economic migrant). Through the establishment of an idealised genuine refugee, consecutive governments have been able to effectively label and categorise who should, or who should not, be a refugee. The following analysis identifies five political processes that position, categorise and castigate them as the other. As such, the chapter presents a narrative of an idealised figure of the refugee that has been constructed through consecutive governments, to the detriment of the refugee.

1. Travel Documentation

The first ascribed characteristic of the genuine refugee is that they will need to have arrived through legal means with the correct travel documentation and visas. Those found travelling without the proper documentation will be banned from travelling and entering the country, or if a carrier such as an airline allows them to travel, that airline can then be fined if they are caught at a later date. The demand for refugees to hold the necessary papers and visas began with the Immigration (Carrier Liabilities) Act of 1987 under Margaret Thatcher's Conservative government. The Act made it illegal for refugees to arrive through modes of travel such as plane or boat without the necessary visa documentation and passports. Reflecting on the Act, Labour MP Jeremy Corbyn (Interview, 2 December 2013) asserted that the government's rationale was that since they 'did not want to and could not get out of the Geneva Convention . . . they introduced the Carriers Liability Act, so that the airline or shipping agents would be financially responsible for anyone who was not subsequently admitted to the country'. With the creation of this Act, only those with valid passports and visas would be eligible to reach Britain, regardless of their refugee status. Without the necessary paperwork, entry into Britain through conventional means such as via airlines and ferries is deemed illegal.

What the Act obscured was that arriving without the proper documents does not mean that the individual is not a refugee. It just means that they are inadequately documented. What the Conservative government did through this legislation was to make arriving without the proper papers a criminal matter that automatically makes claiming asylum without papers very difficult. This is what Ben Bowling and Sophie Westenra (2018: 4) refer to as 'crimmigration', which is the criminalisation of immigration/refugee law.

Labour MP Mike Watson lambasted the Conservative government for its inability to comprehend the contemporary refugee situation:

> The Government . . . fails to understand what is involved in fleeing persecution . . . requiring passengers to provide what is termed 'valid travel documentation' at the point of exit. In many cases, that is simply impossible. Companies are to be instructed to reject anyone travelling on false documents. But how else are people fleeing persecution to leave the country in which they are being persecuted? It is hardly likely that they will be issued with a passport and a neat visa stamp, yet the Home Office appears to think that they are in the same position as someone seeking simply to emigrate from the United Kingdom. That is nonsense. (HC Deb 13, November 1991: vol 198 col 1082)

Despite this, Jack Straw, then New Labour Home Secretary, was still insisting in 2001 at a speech to the Institute for Public Policy Research that the demand for the correct documentation and visas was not impacting on the safety of refugees, arguing 'some may say that the increased use of visas and the imposition of penalties on carriers are the main barriers preventing refugees from reaching safety, and that the answer is therefore to end these policies. I disagree.' Indeed, with the implementation of the Nationality, Immigration and Asylum Act of 2002, it established criminal sanctions for those individuals arriving without the correct, or valid travel documents, thus highlighting the continuing crimmigration of the British refugee system. Indeed, the focus on this criminalisation of movement led the British Refugee Council (cited in Ibrhamin and Howarth 2018b) to publicly state, 'there is a worrying trend within the United Kingdom's asylum procedures of judging an asylum application by looking at how an individual came to claim asylum rather than why they had to flee'.

Indeed, the Carriers Liability Act was strengthened and reinforced when the government introduced Le Touquet Agreement of 2003. This bilateral agreement between Britain and France saw the British border extended to Calais, as well as Britain financing the militarisation of police within and surrounding Calais. With Le Touquet, the British border has been reinforced from the French side, which has had the effect of making passage to Britain harder, with refugees increasingly stuck on the French side, creating a population in waiting. The implementation of Le Touquet 'allows the number of refugees arriving in Britain to remain low by physically extending the hostile environment to Calais'. This means that through both the Carriers Liability Act and the Le Touquet Agreement it is near impossible for refugees to gain access to Britain in order to lodge an asylum appeal (Institute for Race Relations 2017: 22). The 'bad' traveller has effectively been barred from entry, and the blame laid on the individuals themselves. The genuine refugee will have the appropriate papers and documentations, and agreements like Le Touquet or the Carriers Liability Act will not impact on their travel, for they will be able to move freely like the good traveller that they are. The result though has seen a sharp increase in refugees stranded in France who are actively seeking sanctuary in Britain, with no accommodation, access to food or benefits, subsisting off the support of NGOs whilst facing the might of French immigration border police who have been dismantling camps in order to disperse the 'migrant' population.

Indeed, a recent example of the Le Touquet Agreement in action occurred in December 2018, when numerous small boats started to make the crossing from France to Britain, carrying mainly Iranian refugees. Then Home Secretary Sajid Javid (cited in Elgot and Walker 2019) sought to strengthen the border in order to prevent further crossings, first by framing the situation as a 'major incident' and drawing on the politics of labelling immediately to refer to the individuals as illegal migrants. Javid argued it was prudent to ask why so many people were 'choosing to cross the Channel from France to the UK when France itself is a safe country? The widely accepted principle is that those seeking asylum should claim it in the first safe country that they reach – be that France or elsewhere' (Elgot and Walker 2019). Javid went on to state 'if you do somehow make it to the UK, we will do everything we can to make sure that you are often not successful because we need to break that link, and to break that link means we can save more lives' (cited in Schofield 2019). Javid (Home Office, 7 January 2019) asserted in the Commons that whilst the UK has obligations to the genuine refugee, 'we will not stand by and allow reckless criminals to take advantage of vulnerable people'.

What has helped to bolster the Le Touquet Agreement has been the politics of labelling. Reframing the refugee issue in Calais as a migrant issue diminishes British responsibility for the problem. And through the prominent use of the labels of illegal or economic migrant, any potential refugee applicants from this route will find their applications immediately undermined. As such, it works doubly effectively for the government. What we are witnessing here through Le Touquet is the externalisation of first, the British border, but also the British practice of hospitality. In Chapter 4, I will develop this argument further to highlight how in the Mediterranean crisis, Britain has extended this practice of externalisation beyond the EU, in order to manage 'migration' levels and shift their responsibility from the European level, to further 'down stream'.

2. Correct Routes of Travel

This leads us to the second ascribed characteristic of the genuine refugee. The genuine refugee needs to have travelled directly from their country of origin and not have passed through a safe third country. First, although not written into the 1951 Refugee Convention, it has become an assumed norm that refugees should seek protection at the nearest possible location. Indeed, with the European Union's Dublin II Regulations (EU 2003), refugees are only allowed to lodge one asylum claim in order to prevent the supposed practice of 'asylum shopping'. The European state in which the refugee arrives first needs to be the state where the refugee application is lodged. As a result, a refugee cannot travel across or between European states to seek asylum in their preferred state of choice (Hatton 2008), for they will be denied refuge in other EU states automatically, and sent back to the first EU country of entry.

Second, historically, Acts such as the Asylum and Immigration Act (AIA) 1996 and the Immigration and Asylum Act 1999 (IAA) reaffirmed this approach. For instance AIA 1996 allowed the Home Office through statutory instruments, to create 'white lists' of countries in which (it appears) that there is no serious risk of persecution. Additionally, Sections 2 and 3 of AIA sought to establish the safe third country rule – that where a refugee was found to have moved through a safe third country, they would be removed from Britain, without further consideration of their application, and transferred to that country. This policy was reaffirmed in subsequent legislation such as the IAA 1999 and the Nationality, Immigration and Asylum Act 2002 (NIAA), thereby reinforcing the issue of 'safe third countries'.

This approach to safe third countries was reaffirmed in the Asylum and Immigration (Treatment of Claimants, etc.) Act 2004 (AIA), which reasserted that individuals seeking refuge should do so in the first safe country they reach, even though international refugee law makes no such distinction or requirement (Legislation.gov.uk 2004: Section 33). The AIA 2004 stipulated that if the individual seeking refuge had not travelled to Britain directly from their country of origin and had had the opportunity at the border of another country to make an asylum claim and seek protection from another state, then they should be deported to that safe third country in order to seek protection there (Refugee Council 2005). Amnesty International viewed the legislation as a cynical attempt by the government to pass on the responsibility for refugee determination and Dallal Stevens (1998a) referred to it as the erosion of the right to seek asylum.

Despite the condemnation, this element of refugee legislation has been well supported in Parliament over the years. Conservative MP Bowen Wells in early 1992 stated (HC Deb 2 November 1992: vol. 213, col 21),

> It is right that we should take away from those seeking asylum the right to come to this country via a third country. If one is a true political refugee, one should seek asylum only in the country next to the one from which one is fleeing. The idea that people can fly from Sri Lanka, as Tamils did the other day, to Malaysia, to India, to Germany and then to this country to seek political asylum is nonsense.

This position was still being expressed ten years later, with the release of the 2002 White Paper, Secure Borders, Safe Haven. The White Paper spoke of the processes of those arriving in Britain, and argued that there were still a large number of abusive applicants entering the system. It stated:

there is a world of difference between offering sanctuary to those in genuine fear of persecution and allowing asylum seekers to stay simply because the UK is their country of preference. The great majority of those seeking asylum could perfectly reasonably have sought protection at an early stage in their journey. (Secretary of State for the Home Department 2002)

Indeed, in 2010, Conservative MP Philip Hollobone (HC Deb 28 June 2010: col 554) drew upon the genuine refugee, arguing 'surely we should not be giving asylum to people who come to this country via another safe country. Yes, let us give asylum to people who are genuinely fleeing persecution, but not to tourists.' Regarding these 'other' countries, it seems apparent that some British politicians have forgotten the colonial reach of the British empire and the perception of Britain as the 'homeland' for many beyond the country.

3. A Well-Founded Fear

The third criterion applied to distinguish the genuine refugee is that they must be fleeing due to a well-founded fear of persecution as specified in the 1951 Refugee Convention. Having arrived legitimately in Britain, direct from their country of origin, and with the necessary visas and passports, the genuine refugee will have a classic 1951 Convention reason for fleeing. This means that the refugee will have a claim for refuge based upon a well-founded fear of persecution due to race, religion, nationality, political opinion or membership of a particular social group (UN High Commissioner for Refugees 1951 Article 1.A). The genuine refugee needs to be able to demonstrate that their fear of persecution is well-founded, and that they are unable or reluctant to seek protection from their country of origin (UK Border Agency 2011). Crucially, the genuine refugee needs to be able to speak of their persecution in a detailed, consistent and coherent manner in order to be viewed as credible. Indeed, the requirements of the refugee application mean that the refugee needs to have a diary of dates readily available in order to retain and maintain their levels of credibility and reliability within the refugee decision making process (Interview McCormack 2014). Yet, as Conservative

MP Kenneth Baker argued in early 1991, although the element of persecution is central for seeking refuge, most individuals applying do so with unfounded applications. Speaking at a time when Britain was witnessing increased numbers of asylum applications from Tamils, Nigerians and Yugoslavs, Baker (HC Deb 2 July 1991: vol. 194, col 165) insisted that this increase in numbers was not equated to the international unrest witnessed, but rather an abuse of a hospitable system. He insisted:

> Fear of persecution is no longer the dominant element for many asylum seekers. In only a small minority of cases in the United Kingdom are the applicants shown to have a 'well-founded fear of persecution', as required by the terms of the 1951 United Nations convention on refugees. The convention is an instrument of last resort, designed to protect life and liberty from immediate threat. It does not confer an unfettered right to travel the world and settle in the country of one's choice.

Many of the parliamentary debates occurring from 1990 onwards continued with this line of thought espoused by Baker, that refugees were not fleeing persecution, but were merely in search of a better life. Conservative MP Kenneth Clarke (HC Deb 2 November 1992: vol. 213, col 21) argued in a 1992 Commons debate, that 'we must recognise that the growth in asylum applications is in part linked to the fact that anyone who asks for asylum is allowed past the normal immigration controls at our port', with this possibility of entry being a prize in itself to draw people. Then Conservative Home Secretary Michael Howard asserted in 1995 that Britain was perceived as an attractive country for benefits internationally and argued that the lure of benefits meant that the number of genuine refugees was significantly eclipsed by those seeking economic gain. Defending the government stance, Howard argued that:

> For far too many people across the world, this country is far too attractive a destination for bogus asylum seekers and other illegal immigrants. The reason is simple: it is far easier to obtain access to jobs and benefits here than almost anywhere else. (Howard, HC Deb 20 November 1995a: col. 335)

This same view of the abuse of British hospitality was upheld by Conservative MP Mark Wolfson (HC Deb 11 December 1995, vol. 268, ccl. 699–808), who declared 'there can be little doubt that one of the reasons for the dramatic rise in applications to enter the UK . . . is the social security benefits that are available to asylum seekers here'. Again, this acts as another example of a failure to take into consideration crises and conflicts at the international stage, as the root cause of individuals seeking refuge. Indeed, more recently, Prime Minister David Cameron (House of Commons Parliament TV, 2015) speaking on the Mediterranean crisis in June 2015, asserted 'let us be clear the vast majority of people who are setting off into the Mediterranean are not asylum seekers, but people seeking a better life'. With this line of logic, the genuine refugee, with their well-founded fear of persecution, should possess all the necessary and relevant documentation pertaining to their persecution, and should be able to articulate their experiences of persecution in a coherent, detailed and timely manner. Any inconsistencies, or missing documents will cast doubt on their application (McFadyen 2019).

4. The Role of Welfare Benefits

A fourth criterion in the construction of the genuine refugee leads on from the previous point, that the refugee is not driven by welfare benefits or economic aspirations, but rather is solely focused upon seeking a safe haven. As previously noted, many ministers have expressed doubts on the numbers of refugees arriving on the shores of Britain. They have argued that the increase in refugee application claims is connected to economic migrants abusing the refugee process to gain access to the welfare system, with Michael Howard, (HC Deb 11 December 1995b, vol. 268, ccl. 699–808) stating in a 1995 debate that Britain 'must be a haven, not a honey pot'. It was assumed through parliamentary debates that the genuine refugee would be willing to endure hardship through policies such as reduced benefits in kind (e.g. the introduction of vouchers rather than cash), as well as the forced dispersal of asylum seekers.

Indeed, dispersal and the social engineering of asylum seekers was a central component of the IAA 1999, the intention being, as the House of Commons, Home Affairs Committee (2018) confirmed, 'that distribution across the country would prevent any one area providing support to considerably more asylum seekers than other areas', due to the perceived pressures on London and the south east. The Act ensured that refugees would be dispersed 'to areas where there is a greater supply of suitable and cheaper accommodation'.

One local Councillor quoted within the report noted that local councils had a 'moral responsibility' to assist with dispersal (House of Commons, Home Affairs Committee, 2018). However, the policy has instead meant that dispersal is usually to economically and socially disadvantaged areas, with the Welsh Refugee Council (2018) asserting that asylum seekers, through dispersal, were enduring 'sub-standard housing which would not be of an acceptable standard for any other publicly funded accommodation'. Yet, this sub-standard accommodation is perceived still as a temptation for refugees to abuse the system.

This position was highlighted clearly with the implementation of the IAA 1999. Jack Straw, as New Labour Home Secretary, argued at the time that the new legislation was essential so as to be 'less of an incentive for the bogus people to come here'. Deterrence, as well as socially engineered dispersal, was central within the IAA, not the protection of refugees, and has remained, a core practice of the British approach. The objective was to remove any incentives in order to deter presumed economic migrants (Fekete 2001; Friedman and Klein 2008). Welfare benefits, especially, were perceived by the New Labour government and the Conservative Liberal Democrat coalition to be a major pull factor for economic migrants to use the refugee route to enter the country rather than through the traditional channels of entry. Certainly, former New Labour Minister of State for Asylum and Immigration, Barbara Roach (Interview 2012), reflected that due to poor asylum and immigration processes, the British refugee system was overwhelmed with claims for refuge, but stressed that many were unfounded, and people were entering merely for economic rather than 1951 Refugee Convention reasons. Because of this, the genuine refugee was assumed to be able to tolerate further trauma in the quest for sanctuary, unlike their abusive bogus counterparts, with then New Labour Minister of State for Immigration, Citizenship and Counter-Terrorism,

Beverley Hughes (HC Written Statement, 23 February 2004: vol. 418, col. 225w) asserting that 'it is vital to discourage' applicants and to send out a clear message that 'we will not tolerate abuse of the asylum system'.

The apparent lure of benefits features prominently within parliamentary discourse. A prime example is provided by Conservative MP Humphrey Malins. He spoke of the genuine refugee in a 2003 debate (HC Deb 17 December 2003, vol. 415, cc1. 587–620), asserting that 'the genuine asylum seeker arriving here, fleeing persecution, torture and possible death, would, if offered a choice between going back or spending two years in a British prison, opt for prison every time'. Government have presented the genuine refugee applicant as above welfare benefits, as neither interested nor impacted by them. For the genuine refugee, the lure of benefits would not matter; thus, the state reducing benefits and introducing payment in-kind in order to deter would-be abusive claimants would not constitute a barrier for the genuine refugee. This aspect of the genuine refugee has been noticeable throughout the last ten years particularly, with the Conservative Liberal Democrat coalition freezing financial support to asylum seekers at £5.23 per day, arguing in 2013 that the rates were adequate (Harper 2013). Thus, the government asserted that the welfare support of refugees should not be a central priority, and should be actively reduced.

What we see emerging then is a dichotomy between the apparent deserving genuine refugee who is worthy of benefits and the scheming bogus asylum seeker who is focused purely on benefits. This dichotomous labelling has escalated to the point where the government in October 2014 refused to continue funding the search and rescue programme in the Mediterranean. It was perceived to be a 'pull factor' as those who were crossing the Mediterranean and subsequently drowning in trying to reach Europe were viewed as merely seeking to abuse the British system, an act that the government considered should not be encouraged (Baroness Anelay, HL Written Statement, 15 October 2014: col WA41). In the hostile environment generated by government rhetoric, the more deserving the asylum seeker is, the more they should be willing to endure in order to attain safety. This logic operates in the government's favour, with the status of refugee becoming a highly prized, yet exclusive label.

5. A Minority Figure

The final criterion on the construction of the genuine refugee is that they constitute a minority figure in the world of 'migrants'. Despite the fact that the number of asylum seekers that actually make it to the shores of Britain is less than 2 per cent of the world's asylum population (UN High Commissioner for Refugees, UK website), parliamentary debates have constructed the notion that of those arriving, the genuine asylum seeker only accounts for a sub-fraction of that total. This is despite the fact that the top ten countries of origin for asylum seekers to Britain include conflict countries such as Iraq, Eritrea, Pakistan and Iran (UNHCR website). Despite the origins of the refugee, it has been continuously perceived within parliament that the vast majority of people arriving in this country do so with unfounded claims. In a 1992 debate, Conservative MP Iain Duncan-Smith (HC Deb 2 November 1992, vol. 213, ccl. 21–120) asserted that:

> many would-be immigrants have seen asylum as another way around the system. The number of those who have a genuine claim to be here, whether on the grounds of asylum or the other immigration rules, has been distorted by the numbers of bogus asylum seekers. It is they who have put such a strain on our traditional tolerance.

Conservative MP Michael Howard speaking in 1995 argued that 'there are countries that generate large numbers of asylum claims, but few, if any, genuine cases' (HC Deb 11 December 1995b: vol. 268, col 1699–808). Similarly, Conservative MP Nigel Waterson declared in a 1999 debate, that most asylum claims are bogus:

> One thing that we know with certainty is that the great majority of applicants will not turn out to be genuine asylum seekers. Any regime must recognise that the great majority of applicants – who, of course, should be treated courteously and humanely while their applications are being processed, which we hope will be done swiftly – will turn out to be making bogus applications. (HC Deb 16 February 1999: vol. 326, col 37–129)

Genuine asylum seekers are considered to be a minority group, with the vast majority of applicants being charged with abusing the system. This position regarding the unfounded claims within Britain was upheld by former Prime Minister Tony Blair in 2010. Blair reflected that:

> The painful stories of refugees fleeing from Hitler and the Nazis and being turned away produced a right and proper revulsion. The presumption was that someone who claimed asylum was persecuted and should be taken in, not cast out. It was an entirely understandable emotion in the aftermath of such horror. Unfortunately, it was completely unrealistic in the late twentieth century. The presumption was plainly false: the majority of asylum claims were not genuine. (Blair, 2010: 204)

The idealised notion of the refugee was constructed through various pieces of legislation and government debates in parliament, and this has led to a self-fulfilling prophecy. If you assume that the vast majority of applicants are bogus, and define them as such, then they will become bogus through legislation, with the legislation shaping 'the person in the image people have of him' (Becker 1991: 34). The legislation itself perpetuates bogus claimants. By assuming that the vast majority of applicants entering the system are bogus, and by defining the majority of applicants as such, then they will become bogus through the legislation, as the system will only view them as such; the system expects bogus applications, having assumed that only the minority applying are genuine. The legislation itself perpetuates and creates bogus claimants.

Presented as the pinnacle, the genuine refugee has continuously been presented as having had particular experiences, adhering to certain modes of travel and being knowledgeable regarding the national asylum policies. The refugee will have arrived direct from their country of origin and will not have arrived via a (safe) third country. They will have a classic definition of persecution and be able to articulate their story in a detailed and constructive manner. They will also not be interested in welfare benefits and will constitute a small percentage of overall migrant numbers. Those who are unable to meet this specific criterion are castigated as bogus, illegal and failed applicants, intent on abusing the generous welfare entitlements of the British refugee system. It is this framing of the genuine refugee that has dominated asylum policies over the last thirty years. Labour MP Jeremy Corbyn (Interview, 2 December 2013), asserted that the language employed by the government is 'deeply dishonest' because it always carries the assumption that Britain is a wholesome country of asylum, committed to the 1951 Refugee Convention, but at the same time, it is erecting 'huge hurdles' for individuals seeking asylum (Interview, Corbyn, 2 December 2013). Through government debates and legislation on the construction of either the idealised asylum seeker or the bogus asylum seeker, Labour MP Diane Abbott (HC Deb, 12 April 2000, vol. 348, ccl. 426–73,), eloquently noted that 'too often in the debate, on both sides, we speak about asylum seekers as though they were some sort of inanimate object – the burden, the problem, the flood or the swamp. However, they are people.' Interestingly, this is noticeable particularly in recent House of Commons debates with the labelling and positioning of the term refugee.

From examining Hansard records between 1990 and 2018, it is apparent to see the impact of the geographical distance on the use of the label refugee. In House of Commons debates, the refugee is commonly referred to as existing 'out there', beyond Britain, inhabiting an environment that is far away. Within the camps of Zaatari, Syria, Darfur, Palestine – this is where the refugee exists. The refugee does not reside in Britain. Indeed, the geographical distance of the refugee has been reinforced during the Mediterranean refugee crisis when David Cameron (HC Deb 7 September 2015b: vol. 599, col 24) asserted that Britain would accept 20,000 refugees from the camps in Turkey, Lebanon and Syria. Those who have undertaken the journey to Europe are not perceived as genuine asylum seekers or refugees in need. These arguments in particular will be explored further in Chapter 4.

For those seeking refuge in Britain, the term refugee is firmly politicised, with the label itself fractured into inferior, more politically sensitive labels, such as asylum seeker, bogus, abusive, illegal, or more recently, the growing dominance of the economic migrant label. What we are witnessing is the further fracturing of the refugee label, emanating from the host state, into the indistinct label of migrant that subsumes the label of refugee and asylum seeker alongside the migrant label. Yet, even the refugee is still a label in itself that is separated from the ultimate label of citizen. What we can witness here is the argument of Hannah Arendt (2003) when she said that refugees highlight the poverty of human rights and the assumption that states protect human rights. Rather, she asserts, refugees are the 'stateless, rightless scum of the earth' who lack the 'right to have rights'. Refugee law, be it at the national or international level, has developed and evolved as a means of control over the refugee subject, resulting in the rights of the state dominating over the rights of the refugee (Behrman 2018: 1). As Samuel Parker (2018: 1) asserts, the establishment of a hostile environment, where destitution, dispersal and detentions are key factors within the asylum system, has taken precedence over hospitality and welcome.

When examining UK asylum law, Frances Nicholson and Patrick Twomey (1998: 6) argue that it 'cannot honestly be viewed as being other than an incremental erection of hurdles that undermine individuals' opportunity to seek and to enjoy that which is theirs as of right: asylum from persecution'. What this has resulted in is a politics of hospitality where fear of the other abusing the system results in consecutive host governments fracturing the label of refuge, creating an idealised genuine refugee label that a minority will attain, and of which the majority are deemed unworthy. By employing hostility, the state is then able to wield an immense level of power, fracturing the label of refugee in order to protect itself from potential 'parasitical' guests who are perceived to be abusing the hospitality provided.

The Hostile Environment

In exploring further the British construction of the genuine refugee, it is prudent to highlight the 2018 Windrush scandal regarding the hostile environment within Britain as well as to offer a context to Windrush and its significance for this chapter. What has been examined so far can be viewed as the initial frame for what we now call and understand as 'the hostile environment'. 'Windrush' refers to an ocean-going ship, the former SS *Empire Windrush*, that had been decommissioned and whose name has now become synonymous with the migration of Caribbean immigrants to the UK after the Second World War. The *Empire Windrush* herself, as Onyekachu Wambu (1998: 20) states, was 'the first ship bringing home the people of Empire from their peripheral margins to the metropolitan centre itself'. The ship arrived in London in 1948, and the subsequent Windrush generation, which covers a range of individuals with differing legal situations, continued to arrive until 1971. They were viewed at the time as a rather insignificant factor in the movement of people, post-Second World War. Indeed, in a memo written in June 1948 by then Minister for Labour H. W. Hardman (cited in Phillips and Phillips 1998: 68), he set the government approach that '[T]here is no logical ground for treating a British subject who comes of his own accord from Jamaica to Great Britain differently from another who comes to London on his own account from Scotland.' The Windrush generation came to Britain, got jobs and many of them settled, having children themselves – for the Windrush generation, they were British. Yet as Mike Phillips and Trevor Phillips (1998: 68) assert, in later years, the official response to Windrush 'has tended to be characterised according to whatever political purpose is being served'. The narratives towards Windrush have changed in order to suit the needs of the government.

The subsequent Windrush scandal, which emerged in early 2018, for Sile Reynolds (2018: 71) 'exposed the government's brutal treatment of some children of those who arrived on the Empire Windrush'. Indeed, the extent, and full understanding of what became commonly known as the hostile environment policies did not emerge into the public consciousness until the Windrush scandal broke, through a *Guardian* investigation in May 2018. The scandal erupted out of the hostile environment and has shed a harsh light on the wider policies of the UK Home Office and the onus it places on proof and belief within the asylum and immigration system.

The Windrush generation were not claiming asylum but were fighting to have their status formally recognised. However, as a result of the hostile environment policy introduced by Theresa May as Home Secretary, employers, the NHS and landlords are now required to ask for proof of citizenship or immigration status.

The Windrush generation, who arrived from 1948 to 1971, had never before had to prove their position. When they arrived in Britain, their boarding cards were retained by border officials. Commonwealth citizens who arrived before 1973 were entitled to indefinite leave to remain. Indeed, as Francis Webber (2018a: 76) remarks, those who arrived as part of Windrush would have had passports that stated they were British subjects, but with the loss of UK and Colonies citizenship when Caribbean colonies gained independence, this status became redundant, a fact unknown to many, they were British citizens. But, with the implementation of the hostile environment, all the Windrush generation now had was their word that they had arrived as part of the Windrush generation. Indeed, it was revealed when the scandal emerged that their arrival boarding cards had been destroyed by the Home Office in 2010. In most cases this was the only official documentation the Windrush generation had to prove their arrival in Britain.

The Windrush scandal is an excellent example to highlight the intensification of asylum and immigration policies within Britain, as well as a solid illustration of how labelling can operate and work within the refugee and immigration system. A group that had once been accepted, through policies and labelling became a 'suspect group'. Bethan Lant (cited in Institute for Race Relations 2018), a member of Praxis, a community group that has been actively supporting Windrush generation cases, reflected that the environment 'changed around them without notice, or certainly without telling them, and now they are finding that everything has changed and they really get caught out'. The hostile environment has revealed with great clarity how hierarchical labels such as the good immigrant/bad immigrant binary, as well as those other labels such as illegal, failed, bogus or economic, 'have been deployed and weaponised by politicians at different times' (Webber 2018c: 3), with sometimes lethal consequences. The Institute of Race Relations (Athwal 2018) has documented how migrants have been caught within the hostile environment, leading to fatalities such as twenty-three-year-old Darfurian Mustafa Dawood, who died whilst fleeing an immigration raid at his work. He was denied refugee status and therefore denied benefits, so took to working illegally in Newport rather than return to his country of origin.

The Windrush generation, once viewed as the good migrants, were re-labelled and categorised as a threat. The hostile environment and the policies that emerged of 'denial, exclusion, surveillance and enforcement, have turned all foreigners into a suspect population and our society into a nation of border guards, establishing state xeno-racism and nativism as central to government policy' (Webber 2018c). The hostile environment is a policy that the government perceives as putting Britain first. Announced in 2012, the UK Home Secretary Theresa May implemented her plan to create what she termed a 'really hostile environment' for illegal immigrants in the UK, so they would leave the country. In the wake of her announcement, she set up an inter-ministerial 'Hostile Environment Working Group' that was tasked with devising measures which would make life as difficult as possible for undocumented migrants and their families in the UK. The explicit intention was to weaponise total destitution and rightlessness, so as to force migrants without the right to be in the country to deport themselves, at low or no cost to the UK. Through a variety of policies such as restricted visas; relocation and squalid asylum housing; private landlords and agency checks on immigration status; the denial of benefits or support; the entrenchment of racialised views; and the removal of legal aid the government were able to cultivate an environment of 'racism, Islamophobia and nativism' (Webber 2018a: 86) that targeted 'illegal', undocumented immigrants, but also had far reaching consequences. As David Cameron (cited in Tyler 2018), then Prime Minister, asserted, speaking after a dawn raid on illegal immigrants in a house in Slough

> We want an immigration system that puts Britain first and so what we're doing today is a whole series of changes that says to people if you come here illegally we will make it harder for you to have a home, to get a car, to have a job, to get a bank account, and when we find you – and we will find you – we'll make sure you're sent back to the country that you came from . . . if you're here illegally you should go home.

After the Windrush scandal broke, Home Secretary Amber Rudd resigned due to having deliberately misinformed parliament regarding crucial information and figures surrounding the hostile environment. The new Home Secretary, Sajid Javid (Home Office 2019), on taking on the post, quickly altered the labelling of the hostile environment. Javid asserted in May 2018, 'I don't like the phrase hostile. So the terminology is incorrect and I think it is a phrase that is unhelpful . . . It is about a compliant environment and it is right that we have a compliant environment.' So, in trying to diffuse the crisis, the policy of the hostile environment was re-labelled in order for the government to maintain control of the policy itself, as well as redirecting attention from the government back to the refugee, migrant other.

In this regard, as noted in Chapter 2, what we are witnessing here is the politics of labelling in motion. Re-labelling is being practised by the labeller, the dominant group, in order to achieve and maintain their goals. The lesson learned was not to alter the policy, but rather to rename and deflect. Indeed, Caroline Nokes (cited in Webber 2018c: 8), then Immigration Minister, argued that the re-labelled compliant environment policy was an approach that the government did not intend on removing, arguing that 'we believe that they provide an important part of our suite to address illegal immigration'. Nokes (cited in Electronic Immigration Network 2018) further commented that reducing immigration numbers to 'sustainable levels' was 'absolutely imperative' for the government and stressed that 'as part of that, we have a compliant environment, which makes sure that people who are in this country illegally are not entitled to access the benefits and services that those who are here legally can'.

The attack on the Windrush generation was overlooked and ignored, and instead, a redoubling on reducing immigration levels was the overarching narrative emerging from the Home Office. Yvette Cooper MP (cited in Electronic Immigration Network 2018), in challenging the government's response to Windrush, argued against Javid and Nokes, asking,

> does not the Minister recognise that, in Windrush cases, people lost their homes, their residency and citizenship rights, their health care rights and their jobs because the Home Office got decisions wrong and there was no right of appeal and no independent checks and balances?

Cooper stressed that in order for lessons to be learned, the government had to rescind policies that weaponised migrant and asylum groups, as well as specifically restore immigration appeal rights that had been removed in order to streamline the system. They had failed to learn from Windrush, a claim also made by the Joint Select Committee on Human Rights (2018), who noted that 'the Home Office does not appear to have acted like an organisation that had discovered it had made serious mistakes'. Rather, the government had approached the scandal, as the Institute for Race Relations states (Webber 2018b), as 'an unfortunate oversight, brought about by individual carelessness'. Thus, the government's failure to learn lessons simply allowed the policy to continue unhindered.

Due to the hostile environment and its dramatic implications for citizens and migrants within Britain, a Permanent People's Panel Judgement (Transnational Immigration Panel 2018) on the hostile environment was established. Convened by experts and advisors on immigration and asylum, the panel found

> deliberate, planned and systematic expression of repressive policies which, translated into legal provisions and norms, affect the full spectrum of the concrete rights which must be recognised in all human beings: rights to life, to dignity, to health, to work, to education.

The PPPJ found that that the Conservative government's policy of hostility was a deliberate 'non-recognition of migrants and refugees as people and members of society despite the disparate nature of their origins and the causes of their migration, displacements and expulsions'. Significantly, the Joint Committee for Human Rights (2018) concluded that there was inadequate regard for human rights by the Home Office.

Indeed, there was a deliberate blanket, homogenous approach adopted through the hostile environment, treating all migrants and refugees as equal, without attention to history, context and individual experiences. Through the creation of the hostile environment, which, Francis Webber (2018a,b,c) argues, has been a long term British approach to asylum and immigration that was intensified during the Conservative Cameron and May premierships, the British government implemented

> an ever deeper and more pervasive political, juridical and cultural transformation of a society which accepts and promotes the reversal of the values of democracy, of binding obligations for Governments and of basic principles of international law as affirmed and enforced in the corresponding international instruments. (Webber 2018a)

The extent and depth of the hostile environment policies within Britain, has been said to highlight an overt 'retreat from universality in human rights' (Webber 2018c). The PPPJ found that the nature of the policies and the fundamental undermining of the individual, who was transformed from the good migrant into an illegal enemy, 'other, aliens, potential or real enemies, invaders and aggressors, both in attitude and in concrete behaviours such as labour contracts, reproduces categories of colonialism and slavery' (Transactional Immigration Panel 2018). The power of the hostile environment, as Reynolds (2018: 71) stressed, was in its 'blunt application' and the basic assumptions that the perceived non-white other was foreign, unlawful and needed to prove their status at all levels of their life, be it work, housing or health care.

Conclusion

Philip Marfleet (2006: xii) raised the question as to why yesterday's 'deserving refugee' has become the 'menacing and unwelcome alien' of today. However, this chapter has underlined how today's refugee is the same as yesterday's refugee: unwelcome and viewed with suspicion by the host state. In reflecting on the manner of the British asylum process, this chapter has sought to examine how the politics of hospitality and the language of labelling have resulted in the creation of an idealised genuine refugee that has allowed the label of refugee to be fractured into inferior sub-categories, further removing the guest refugee from the sanctuary sought. Concentrating on the period since 1990, the chapter highlights that although Britain is a signatory to the 1951 Convention, it has at the same time always maintained a precarious relationship with the refugee. Through identifying five ways in which successive governments since 1990 have sought to fracture the label of the refugee (travel through legal means, travelled directly from country of origin, fleeing for a well-founded reason of persecution, not driven by welfare and finally that the refugee is a minority group), the chapter has identified the politics of labelling at work within the British refugee system, at the expense of the refugee. Hospitality has always been a policy that has been asserted by British governments, but in reality, the process of refuge in Britain reflects the notion of hostipitality: with hospitality and hostility very much being two sides of the same coin operating within the British refugee system. The recent Windrush scandal stands as testament to the structural hostility in place in order to reduce immigration.

With the establishment of the idealised genuine refugee, consecutive British governments have been able to create a self-fulfilling prophecy regarding the abuse of the system. The host, by initiating policies and legislation that have identified accepted behaviours and experiences of a genuine asylum seeker, the construction of an idealised asylum seeker has emerged at the expense of those not able to meet the criteria, through no fault of their own. This labelling has allowed consecutive governments since 1990, through the politics of labelling, to castigate the majority of asylum claimants as bogus, abusive, illegal or simply economic migrants. Or, as the Windrush scandal identified, through the re-labelling of a good migrant group, a whole subset of the population, through the machinery of the hostile environment and the politics of labelling, found the state weaponised against them – barred from work, health care, education and benefits.

By setting the bar for refuge (and immigration) so high, the vast majority of those arriving will automatically be denigrated and shaped into inferior labels of asylum. The process of labelling the genuine refugee, in this regard, operates in the state's interest, highlighting the political nature of labelling. By fragmenting the label of the refugee, consecutive British governments since 1990 and regardless of political leanings have been able to implement policies that strike at the heart of the asylum system by asserting that they are protecting themselves as well as the genuine asylum seeker from the growing hordes of abusive claimants. This is where we can see how the hostile environment potentially is a long term policy in operation in Britain that was intensified under the watch of the

Conservative government (2010 onwards). Yet, the hostile environment is just another label itself. For the conditional hospitality and the extreme practice of hostipitality are manifestations of xenophobia, where fear of the other and abuse of the system operate. This is how the 1951 Refugee Convention has operated in Britain, but as James Hathaway (1991: 180) notes, this is how the Convention has always operated – with the needs of states first, noting that the Convention is a 'facade of universal humane concern'. State sovereignty within the international refugee regime is paramount. This facade of hospitality needs to be challenged, for although Britain is still engaging in the refugee process and upholding the 1951 Refugee Convention, the notion of unconditional hospitality is not the model to which they aspire. Rather hostipitality is in operation, whereby fear of the other abusing the system (and the host state) is resulting in stringent policies that are detrimentally affecting those individuals seeking sanctuary in Britain. Or, as in the case of Windrush, re-labelling groups of citizens, and denying rights.

The next chapter will engage with the second case study of the book, examining how this process of hospitality, facilitated by the politics of labelling, has been externalised beyond the state of Britain during the Mediterranean crisis. The chapter examines the projection of the politics of hospitality and labelling far beyond the territorial confines of the state in order to contain and curtail British responsibility during the Mediterranean refugee crisis. It analyses how the figure of the refugee is geographically re-labelled when they enter into the region of Europe, transforming from a refugee to an (illegal) economic migrant, thereby creating hierarchies of need within the crisis that operate in the state interest.

CHAPTER 4

British Political Labelling of the Refugee during the Mediterranean Crisis

We have a proud history of relieving the distressed and helping the vulnerable – whether it's through our military, our diplomacy, our humanitarian work or our support for refugees, let us continue this tradition. Let Britain stand up for the displaced, the persecuted and the oppressed. For the people who need our help and protection the most, let Britain be a beacon of hope. (May 2015b)

The Syrian crisis has seen the largest movement in recent history of people entering into Europe, many risking their lives to travel by boat across the Mediterranean in search of sanctuary. The conflict has generated over 5 million refugees, with a further 7 million internally displaced – 12 million people in total are affected by the crisis as of 2019, with Syrians forced to flee persecution and conflict in their home country, many escaping to camps or urban centres within Turkey, Lebanon or Jordon, with a minority (roughly 10 per cent) undertaking the journey west, towards Turkey and onwards to Europe (UNHCR 2016b). Of those people entering into the EU seeking sanctuary, Syrians represent roughly 50 per cent of arrivals, but they are not the only individuals displaced; for example, 20 per cent of EU arrivals hail from Afghanistan and 15 per cent from Iraq, all refugee producing countries. Indeed, the crisis is not just a Syrian one, albeit it has been framed as such. Rather we are witnessing multiple emergencies from three different continents. As 2015 progressed and Europe witnessed an unprecedented rise in asylum and migration movements into and across Europe, the British government found themselves slowly and reluctantly embroiled within what has been termed the Mediterranean crisis, the European crisis, or in the words of Alison Phipps (2019), a 'crisis of reception'.

However, a geographical distinction has emerged in relation to the labelling of these individuals – especially when they enter into European territory. The framing of the debate that emerged surrounding the Mediterranean crisis has focused on the labelling of these individuals. Who are they? What are their intentions? Why are they travelling? What do they seek? One of the labels that has come to dominate within the British narrative, be it within the government or media rhetoric, has been the label of migrant. The crisis has been framed as one of migration. These are 'migrants' undertaking the journey, even when we can clearly identify those individuals undertaking the journeys and place their country of origin and might otherwise be referring to them as refugees or asylum seekers instead. The politics of labelling became central to the Mediterranean crisis response. Be it the response of the British government, the media or the European Union, the politics of labelling has become a central political tool within the Mediterranean crisis. Through labelling, states have been able to denote political authority, political responsibility, as well as the application of international refugee law or national migration law. Through the politics of labelling, I argue that a geographical hierarchy of need has emerged within the Mediterranean crisis, with those individuals entering into the European Union being re-labelled from refugees to migrants, thereby invoking alternative levels of state responsibility as well as differing levels of law. For instance national laws on migration rather than international refugee law and its accompanying responsibilities.

The chapter will apply an analysis of the framework of labelling and hospitality to the Mediterranean crisis, in order to highlight and critique the British approach to the crisis. As well as employing the theoretical framework of labelling and hospitality, the chapter draws upon Hansard archival material, analysing parliamentary debates on the Syrian and Mediterranean refugee crisis between 2011 and 2018. It examines the labelling of the crisis, and charts how the British government has sought to create a label of refugee that is bound by geographical constraints, and how this is an approach that is not tied to party politics, instead following a non-partisan logic within the House of Commons. The chapter begins by examining how labelling operates within the British response to the refugee crisis, observing the domination of the migrant label. The chapter then discusses the significance of the refugee camps, as well as how to understand distant suffering in the context of the British response to the European refugee crisis. The emphasis is very much on the language and labelling employed in order to geographically frame and conceptualise the Mediterranean crisis and externalise the British response, beyond the sphere of Europe.

In doing so, the chapter specifically addresses the practice of externalised humanitarian hospitality – the framework developed from Chapter 1 – and argues that the Mediterranean crisis and the British response to it is a prime example of externalised humanitarian hospitality, whereby hospitality is projected beyond the confines of the territorial state, under the guise of humanitarian support. Through declaring humanitarian aid for only the most vulnerable in the designated region, states such as Britain are able to control and contain the crisis, whilst simultaneously upholding their humanitarian credentials. The politics of labelling facilitated this externalisation of hospitality as the refugee label itself is geographically externalised from Britain, creating a hierarchy of suffering.

Britain, Labelling and the Mediterranean Crisis

Within the Mediterranean crisis there has been a subconscious focus on the labelling and language employed in order to frame the crisis. The labels of migrant and refugee have often been used interchangeably by the British government, with the migrant label, particularly that of the economic migrant, taking precedence within the government. Indeed, the crisis has often been referred to as the migrant crisis, implying that a crisis of economic migration is upon us; however, the labels are remarkably different. There is a crucial distinction between what these labels are entitled to, with different levels of assistance and protection under national and international law. The blurring of the labels, as the UNHCR (2016c) argues, takes attention away from the specific legal protection requirements of refugees. In contrast to refugees, who are not able to return safely home, returning home is not generally a problem for migrants – if they wish to return home, they will continue to receive protection from their country of origin. This distinction is important, for immigration is handled through a series of varying policies and legislation implemented at the national level. In comparison though, international or regional law is invoked by states when dealing with refugees. States within the EU have an international as well as a regional responsibility for anyone seeking refuge in their country, due to having ratified the 1951 United Nations Convention Relating to the Status of Refugees. But, by using the label of migrant, as Britain prefers to do, Britain has been able to obscure, if not deny, specific legal protections that refugees are internationally entitled to.

The rhetoric emanating from the British government since the Mediterranean crisis started to dominate political discussions has centred on the fact that events that we have been witnessing are due to an upsurge in economic migrants seeking a better way of life, using fractured as well as metaphorical language to engage, as well as to deflect the crisis. We see rhetoric emerging from the government that labels the crisis purely in terms of economic migration, as well as drawing on language that dehumanises. This has been a common theme within refugee policy in British politics, whereby the emphasis has been on one of reduction and prevention, and the setting of ever higher standards of protection (McFadyen 2016). Words matter, labels matter, and how we label someone not only impacts on their position, but also our interactions and responsibilities towards them. Labelling does not occur within a political vacuum – and this really needs to be stressed, for the creation, application and utilisation of labels is always political. It is, to recall Geof Wood's (1985) words, the 'act of politics involving conflict as well as authority'. Labelling is a conscious decision by one group to label another – shaping and normalising behaviours whilst establishing distinctions between individuals, normally to the detriment of the labelled; as Wood (1985) asserts, 'it is a relationship of power, asymmetrical and one-sided'. Certainly, as David Turton (2003) notes, the language of migration is not innocent. With the

Mediterranean crisis, we are regularly inundated with statistics, data and figures. Such analysis of the crisis has reduced it to abstract figures and numbers, thus establishing a homogenous narrative whilst the 'messier vicissitudes of individualized experience (pain, suffering, loss and also resourcefulness, ability, etc.) are left by the wayside' (Gupte and Mehta 2007: 64).

In the emergence of the Mediterranean crisis, and following the Lampedusa mass tragedies in April 2015, British Prime Minister David Cameron (cited in BBC News 30 July 2015b) asserted that we 'have got a swarm of people coming across the Mediterranean, seeking a better life, wanting to come to Britain because Britain has got jobs, it's got a growing economy, it's an incredible place to live'. The following month Cameron again asserted that those people entering into Europe 'are economic migrants and they want to enter Britain illegally, and the British people and I want to make sure our borders are secure and you can't break into Britain without permission'. Indeed, the government was so convinced that the people entering the Mediterranean were only migrants it had declared the previous year, in October of 2014, that it was pulling funding on future search and rescue programmes in the Mediterranean Sea. Announced in a written statement to the House of Lords by Lady Anelay (House of Lords, Written Statement, 15 October 2014), the statement read:

> We [the government] do not support planned search and rescue operations in the Mediterranean. We believe that they create an unintended 'pull factor', encouraging more migrants to attempt the dangerous sea crossing and thereby leading to more tragic and unnecessary deaths.

This narrative of the crisis merely being one of migration continued into 2016. In January 2016, David Cameron (cited in *The Guardian* 27 January 2016) in a response during Prime Ministers Questions argued that the residents of the Jungle camp in Calais, France, were merely a 'bunch of migrants' wanting to come to Britain.

From the government's position, the Mediterranean crisis was not a refugee crisis. These individuals entering into the EU were not invoking international refugee law or the spirit of humanitarianism. They required neither protection nor security and the emphasis was placed on national state approaches, as well as reduction and prevention. This rhetoric of the Mediterranean crisis as being solely a matter of economic migrants was reinforced by the British government when they eventually agreed to accept 20,000 refugees over a five year period in September 2015. This was largely in response to a summer of news reports of shipwrecks and large scale loss of life in the Mediterranean, culminating with three-year-old Syrian Alan Kurdi's lifeless body making the international press, having drowned in attempting to reach Greece. Kurdi ignited a grassroots social response across Europe, particularly in Britain, where movements such as Solidarity for Refugees were born, in direct opposition to the perceived lack of action by the British government. The movement though was a rallying against the disconnected and dehumanising language of migration that was being employed to frame the crisis (Ereira 2015). Indeed, David Cameron continued to reinforce the narrative of the crisis as one of migration. Speaking to the House of Commons on 7 September 2015, Cameron (2015b) argued that:

> 300,000 people have crossed the Mediterranean to Europe so far this year. These people came from different countries under different circumstances. Some are economic migrants in search of a better life in Europe; many are refugees fleeing conflict. It is vital to distinguish between the two. (HC Deb, 7 September, vol. 599, col. 23)

Conservative MP Bernard Jenkins argued in June 2015 (HC Deb 8 June 2015, vol. 595, col. 906) that it was morally wrong for refugees to be arriving in Britain seeking asylum, and charged that Britain was a beacon for those claiming human rights. Jenkins asked

> why do clandestines cross continents of free countries to claim asylum here? While we must honour our obligations under the tightly defined criteria for asylum claims laid down in the 1951 Geneva Convention, how much does the way that we adjudicate on the much wider provisions of the European Convention on human rights unreasonably inflate asylum claims so that the UK attracts people to claim asylum here rather than elsewhere, and what should be done about it?

The government were making a clear linguistic distinction in regards to the crisis. This was a crisis of migration. Some refugees were caught up in the process, but primarily, the movement of people entering into the EU was down to the quest for increased economic security, and a clear distinction between the two separate groups was essential. Cameron (HC Deb 7 September 2015b, vol. 599. col. 23) went on to state that 'clearly there are people who have been crossing the Mediterranean – particularly those coming from Libya on the central Mediterranean route – who are economic migrants in search of a better life'. The government felt that the refugee was not the central issue within the Mediterranean crisis. As then Home Secretary Theresa May (HC Deb 24 June 2015a, vol. 597, col. 902) asserted in June 2015:

> Reports about what is happening in Calais and about people crossing the Mediterranean often use the terms such as 'refugee' or 'asylum seeker' to describe all those people, although, as we know, a significant proportion of them are economic migrants who are trying to enter Europe illegally. We think it important to break that link, so that people are made aware that they cannot make those journeys, arrive in Europe illegally, and settle here.

When the government agreed to accept 20,000 refugees in September 2015 and provide five years of humanitarian protection to each individual, they were at the same time offering a (potentially limited) humanitarian solution to the crisis stressing that the central issue was not one of refuge. This was further confirmed by the condition that the 20,000 refugees would only be accepted from camps surrounding Syria, Turkey, Lebanon or Jordan. The government would not be accepting individuals for refuge from within the EU itself. The same geographical principle was applied when the British government sought to provide resettlement for 3,000 children in May 2016 through the Dubs Amendment, but again, preference was given to those external to the EU, from North Africa and the Middle East, as those who had entered into the EU were viewed as undeserving and it was feared that it would lead to a 'perverse incentive' of families encouraging their children to head to Europe, unaccompanied (Cameron cited in BBC News 4 May

2016). This is the geographical externalisation of humanitarian hospitality – humanitarianism, but conditional. The externalisation of hospitality highlights the upholding of welcome whilst at the same time 'the shunning of the uninvited' closer to the British state (Mountz and Briskman 2012: 23).

The rhetoric surrounding the Mediterranean crisis is one that is entrenched in the politics of labelling, be it from the language employed by the European Union and the framing of the crisis as one of migration, through states such as Britain and the rhetoric employed here. The individuals seeking refuge are labelled, generally through a negative, derogatory and dehumanising employment of language that presents the other as an unwelcome parasitical guest. The language and vocabulary in operation within the Mediterranean crisis regarding the refugee does vary in its range from state to state, or the EU itself, but the language is 'singular in its intention', as Roger Zetter (2007: 184) asserts, 'to convey an image of marginality, dishonesty, a threat, unwelcomed'. This has been a central framework applied to the Mediterranean crisis, and the 'search for a better life' has been reduced to purely economics and notions of settlement, without a more nuanced lens of forced migration being employed (David Cameron, HC Deb, 7 September 2015a, vol. 599, col. 38).

For the framing of the other as an economic migrant does not focus on how the other could positively contribute to society or to our economies, but rather on how they are cheating the system, breaking in, stealing or devaluing the workforce. Importantly the label of economic migrant also fails to account for the potential hardship and suffering experienced by the individual (Michalski 2015), viewing migration simply as a pull factor, rather than a push factor, or as forced migration. The identification applied to those individuals fails to extend further than acknowledging that they have come from a migrant route via Libya. There has been a systematic failure to engage with the fragility of life in Libya, both for Libyans and for refugees/migrants there. There appears to be a failure to acknowledge the closing of safe routes, in and through the country, or the movement of people within the African continent itself, or the conflicts and socio-political insecurity faced by millions across the continent that have forced them to seek refuge and economic prospects further north, or in Europe. Particularly, individuals forced from the Horn of Africa, the Democratic Republic of Congo or South Sudan, for instance, who face conflict or severe political repression (Eaton 2017; Squire 2017). The socio-political origins of those undertaking the southern Mediterranean journey remain unspoken, if not silenced, and presented simply as journeys of migration. As the report by Heaven Crawley et al. (2016) stressed, 'there has been little or no interest in the "back stories" of those arriving: instead the gap between someone leaving their home country and his or her arrival in Europe has been filled with generalisations and assumptions'. As such they are framed as a threat to our way of life. This is despite recent longitudinal research in to the Mediterranean crisis by Crawley et al. (2016) which has reported that up to 77 per cent of those sampled for the study 'explicitly mentioned factors that could be described as forced migration, including conflict, persecution, violence, death threats and human rights abuse'. By labelling these people simply as economic migrants, Britain is able to sideline her international responsibility. David Cameron (HC Deb 3 June 2016a, vol. 596, col. 583) continued to reinforce the framing of individuals from the southern Mediterranean routes as merely migrants when he asserted that 'the vast majority of people who are setting off into the Mediterranean are not asylum seekers but people seeking a better life. Our role should be . . . sorting out the situation in Libya, turning back the boats where we can'. The emphasis was on pre-emptive pull-backs from Libya, regarding the individuals on the boats. The simplistic response was that if you stop the boats, you stop the crisis.

At the Conservative Party conference in 2015, Theresa May (2015b) stressed the legality of the journey that these individuals were undertaking, emphasising the legal and security concerns raised by the movement of these individuals. May asserted that allowing individuals to claim refuge in Britain, 'encourages vulnerable people to take dangerous and illegal journeys to get here'. This then benefits the smugglers and traffickers who can capitalise on the movement of the people, resulting in only the wealthiest and strongest being able to eventually access asylum in Britain. This is despite the United Nations Convention and Protocol Relating to the Status of Refugees asserting through Article 31 (UNHCR 2006) that no contracting state 'shall impose penalties, on account of their illegal entry or presence, on refugees . . . coming directly from a territory where their life or freedom was threatened'. Furthermore, it was legislation such as the Carrier's Liability Act 1987, the Asylum and Immigration (Treatment of Claimants) Act 2004 or the Dublin Regulations II (EU 2003), brought in by the British government and the EU, that legalised certain routes that refugees could take through safe, legal routes as well as cracking down on visa requirements. For instance, visas were introduced for Syrian nationals in March 2012 in response to the developing crisis, which was then extended in March 2015 in order to 'protect the UK's national and border security' (McGuiness 2017).

Indeed, a dichotomy was created between the financial cost of fleeing and refugeehood, with only economic migrants being viewed as being financially savvy enough to undertake the journey to Europe. Adam Holloway (HC Deb 8 Dec 2015, vol. 599, col. 268), MP for Gravesham argued that

> the current migrants are overwhelmingly working-age males who have paid a hefty price to make the trip. Most of the countries they came from are certainly poor, but they are not at war. It costs thousands to board a smuggler's boat and a lot of money in the months before to travel to it.

The House of Commons agreed on the 14 December 2015 that the focus of the British approach to the crisis would be to address current migratory pressures that focused on 'shorter and longer term actions to break the business model of people smugglers and traffickers, to break the link between rescue at sea and permanent settlement in the EU, and to address the root causes of migrants' journeys' (J. Brokenshire, HC Deb 14 Dec 2015, vol. 603). Through the use of the migrant label, followed then by the emphasis on smugglers and traffickers, the government were redirecting the attention of the crisis away from the figure of the refugee in what Adrian Little and Nick Vaughan-Williams (2016: 546) have termed a 're-problematisation of the problem as being one of criminality'. Interestingly, the government chose to use language of compassion and humanity when engaging with the migrant label, due to the larger gravity of the situation, but the end result was that migrants were unwelcome and could seek no support from Britain. The crisis then could be framed as one of migration, of individuals seeking a better way of life and of smugglers and traffickers who were capitalising on these movements and willingly putting individual lives at risk. Stopping the boats would save lives; thus the humanitarian angle.

The construction of the refugee as migrant has continued throughout the crisis, with the British refugee system perceived as an appealing process that merely incentivises individuals to take hazardous journey for financial and personal gain, rather than humanitarian concern. Jacob Rees-Mogg stressed that

> The refugees who come are not the helpless and the lame, but the fittest and the most able to take the risks involved in trying to cross the sea to come to the European Union. We have seen that 70% of the refugees who have come to the European Union are in fact men, primarily young men. A system has been set up that creates incentives and leads people to take foolish risks to come here in the first place. The people who are most at risk – the children, the elderly and the frail – are left behind, because if they apply from their risky country, the forces of the EU will not let them in. (HC Deb 14 December 2015, col. 1347)

Yet, as Justine Greening, then Secretary of State for International Development, argued, the government needed to keep their response humane: 'we need to see the people behind many of the statistics that we read in the paper . . . They are literally putting their lives on the line to get a better life, and we should never forget the stories of the people behind those terrible numbers' (HC Deb 3 June 2015, col. 574). Push-back against the dominant migration rhetoric was present, with MPs calling on humanitarian and humane language to be employed, as well as invoking a moral responsibility to respond. In the words of Peter Grant (HC 14 December 2015, vol. 603, col. 1365):

> it continues to create an impression that a significant number of these 4 million desperate citizens are trying to come here because they are attracted to living in the United Kingdom. They are not; they are trying to get out of Syria because they do not want to die. I just wish that the

terminology that has been used and the language of this debate would recognise that this is a crisis that has fundamentally been caused by war, violence and civil unrest. It has not been caused by an economic miracle happening in the United Kingdom or Germany.

Labelling then is highly political by nature and through the production and implementation of labels (consecutive) British governments have been able to define the agenda regarding refuge, particularly in the Mediterranean crisis. Labelling in this regard has provided the government with the power to redefine the notion and legality of refuge in Britain, as well as to protect the label of refugee from the perceived abuse by those displaced by the Mediterranean crisis. Only the most vulnerable are worthy of the label of refugee. As the 2017 Conservative Manifesto (2017) asserted, 'wherever possible, the government will offer asylum and refuge to people in parts of the world affected by conflict and oppression, rather than to those who have made it to Britain'. A clear geographical distinction in hospitality has emerged, prioritising those individuals who are geographically distant from Britain, in a policy move that protects the British state from unauthorised entries but at the same time, both diminishes as well as maintains British international responsibility. The Mediterranean crisis is a crisis of migration, not of refuge, and the British response is to project humanitarian hospitality beyond the EU, directly to the crisis regions themselves.

The Significance of the Camps

In establishing the policy of resettling 20,000 Syrian refugees, David Cameron set out on the 7 September 2015b (HC Deb, vol. 599, col. 24) the government position, confirming that 'we will continue to show the world that this is a country of extraordinary compassion, always standing up for our values and helping those in need'. The British approach sought to 'provide refugees with a more direct and safe route to the United Kingdom, rather than risking the hazardous journey to Europe, which has tragically cost so many lives' (Cameron, HC Deb, 7 September 2015b, vol. 599, col. 24). In pledging to accept up to 20,000 refugees over a five year period, Steven Kirkwood (2017: 116) notes that Cameron was employing a process of humanisation, of 'constructing people as belonging to a common moral community, of acting in ways that are understandable, and as deserving of support'. Indeed, Kirkwood notes that from 2015 to 2016 there was an increase in positive statements regarding refugees in the public and political sphere. Yet, the positivity and humanisation was directed to those external to the European Union, to the Syrian refugees residing within the camps in Syria, Jordan, Lebanon or Turkey – that is where the refugee resides. As Sherene Razack (2008: 101) reminds us, 'most politicians define themselves as tolerant and fair-minded, and as opponents of colonialism and racism, the language of control is masked by the language of humanitarian values and economic rationalism'.

It is important to remember that Britain has been providing over one billion pounds in aid to Syria and its surrounding neighbours in response to the Syrian crisis, but this again reinforces the argument being developed here that the refugee, and even the crisis itself, is based on a geographical understanding that is external to the EU. The government are not engaged in providing aid within the European region, but instead are prioritising their response external to the region in what Nick Vaughan-Williams (2015: 18) terms 'bordering practices under the rubric of humanitarianism'. This is where we see the change in language from the right to leave to the right to remain, with refugees encouraged to stay within their country of origin by providing assistance to them there, rather than having them seek protection through asylum across an international border. Those individuals who have undertaken the journey to the EU in search of refuge, rather than maintaining their refugee, or even asylum seeker label, undergo a transformation into an (economic) migrant on entering into the EU zone. By entering the territory of the European Union, these refugees become individuals who are unwelcome and perceived as a threat to European culture, values and economic security, with the agenda developing that these individuals need to be deterred at all costs. This practice of externalisation is a process common at the EU level where externalisation and extra-territorialisation of governance is projected (Bialasiewicz 2012: 846) stretching the borders of the EU. Indeed, externalising the refugee has been viewed as part of the norms and standards of the EU neighbourhood approach, that the refugee should reside at a distance (Bialasiewicz 2012: 852).

This is not a unique approach to refugee politics at the international level. Indeed, this is a practice favoured by the Australian government where hospitality is projected externally, manifesting in the Pacific solution, where refugees are removed geographically to off-shore Island centres like Naura and Manus Island. Refugees are prevented from arriving at Australia's territory. Instead, they are housed in off-shore detention centres, thus limiting access to judicial processes, whilst upholding humanitarian concern (Mountz 2011: 121). Indeed, it is important to remember, that British practices of externalised hospitality can be traced back to the 'off-shore' proposals that were discussed by New Labour back in 2003. These proposals were to establish external asylum centres with the intention of assessing claims in situ before refugees began their hazardous journey. This is what Jennifer Hyndman (2003: 168) calls the language of humanitarian assistance, 'a highly spatialized project of reorientating human displacement closer to home'.

British practices of refuge have been so constrained and negated throughout the refugee crisis that practices of hospitality have ended up being geographically positioned far beyond the territorial location of first, the British state but second, the European Union, in order to minimise, contain but crucially uphold hospitality. It is still present, but under extreme conditions whereby hostipitality is practised. The refugee through externalised humanitarian hospitality is known by the British state 'only in terms of how they might be contained, policed and regulated' (Razack 2008: 92). For the British host, in order to protect the practices of hospitality from the 'parasitical guest', has gone as far as to cease partaking in the act of hospitality altogether. Within the Mediterranean crisis, those individuals who have entered the EU have been framed by the British government as not requiring assistance, being labelled as migrants or perceived to be in 'safe third countries'. A re-labelling process has occurred by which, when refugees geographically enter Europe, they are transformed from refugees to (illegal, economic) migrants. For Britain, hospitality is not required in this context; it can be denied to these individuals and instead externalised to the individuals who reside in the camps surrounding Syria. This is where hospitality should be practised and, through government narratives and labelling, this is where the genuine refugee resides. As Cameron (HC Deb, 29 January 2014, vol. 574, col. 851) affirmed when pledging to assist in the crisis, 'we will be coming forward with a scheme to help the most needy people in those refugee camps and offer them a home in our country. We want to make sure that we particularly help those who have been victims of sexual violence'.

The narrative of the camps and the British response emerged quickly in reaction to the Mediterranean crisis. By drawing a demarcating line between those internal and external to the EU, the Conservative government have been able to establish a narrative of humanitarianism that is rooted solely in the geographical proximity to Syria. David Cameron (HC Deb, 29 June 2015a), speaking in June 2015, made a clear distinction as to where British responsibility should reside, asserting:

> We are drawing a distinction between resettling the most vulnerable refugees who are outside the European Union, for instance in Syrian refugee camps, for whom we think Britain can do more and – this where I think the European Union is potentially heading down the wrong track – a relocation programme for migrants who are already within the EU.

It is important to note that within this quote alone, Cameron engages with the notion of vulnerability, but also that there is a geographical distinction between refugees internally and externally to the EU. He does this clearly by adopting alternate labels of refugee (externally) and migrant (internally) to reinforce where the crisis is located as well as to identify where British responsibility should lie, in addition to supporting a geographical hierarchy of need with the 'most vulnerable' situated externally. For instance, the establishment of the Syrian Vulnerable Person Resettlement Programme (VPRP) in 2015 saw the British government create a route for Syrians to settle in the country, with a priority placed upon the most vulnerable, such as the elderly, the disabled, victims of sexual violence and torture. The VPRP was created to parallel the UNHCR quota resettlement programme that was in operation at the European Union level, but by operating a separate system, Britain was able to abstain from the EU quota scheme that had been implemented, whilst at the same time upholding a UNHCR approved 'durable solution' to the refugee crisis (McGuinness 2017: 7). David Cameron (HC Deb 7 September 2015b, col. 24), speaking to the House of Commons on 7 September 2015, set out the plan, asserting:

> given the scale of the crisis and the suffering of the Syrian people, it is right that we should do much more. We are proposing that Britain should resettle up to 20,000 Syrian refugees over the rest of this Parliament. In doing so, we will continue to show the world that this is a country of extraordinary compassion, always standing up for our values and helping those in need. Britain will play its part alongside our European partners, but because we are not part of . . . the EU's borderless Schengen agreement or its relocation initiative, Britain is able to decide its own approach. We will continue with our approach of taking refugees from the camps, and from elsewhere in Turkey, Jordan and Lebanon. This provides refugees with a more direct and safe route to the United Kingdom, rather than risking the hazardous journey to Europe, which has tragically cost so many lives.

The government heavily resisted the EU resettlement quota or relocation of 'migrants' with then Home Secretary Theresa May (cited in The Mediterranean Migrant Crisis, 2015) arguing that it would only 'strengthen the incentives for criminal gangs to keep plying their evil trade'. Or else it was argued that the UNHCR resettlement programme was merely 'tokenistic' in light of the sheer scale of the crisis and that rather, the key response was to provide humanitarian aid within the region alone (McGuinness 2017: 9). This hesitation towards EU quotas though was replicated by other EU states. Spanish Foreign Minister Jose Manuel Garcia-Margallo argued that calls for solidarity needed to be 'proportionate, just and realistic' and stressed that due to the country's double digit unemployment levels, offering hospitality to refugees would be 'bad service' domestically (The Guardian). France, the Czech Republic, Estonia, Hungary, Latvia, Lithuania, Poland and Slovakia all opposed the quota system. As Cameron argued, assisting at the EU level was not a viable position for Britain to be adopting. Cameron's (HC Deb, 7 September 2015b, vol. 599, col. 64) approach was that

> Those people who have made it already to Europe are in many cases in a far better and much safer situation than the people still stuck in Syria or stuck in the refugee camps, which is why it is those people whom our effort will be directed towards.

Indeed, Cameron (HC Deb, 7 September 2015b, vol. 599, col. 39) stressed that

> we do not believe it is right to take part in the European relocation quota because we think that a better answer for Britain, which is such a major investor in the refugee camps, is to take people directly from the camps . . . By taking a long-term view and looking at the asylum seekers we have taken and the people we have resettled from around the world, I would say Britain is absolutely fulfilling our moral responsibility, and we absolutely play our part.

Finally, he noted that he did not

> believe the right answer is for Britain to take people who have already arrived in Europe. We think that it is better to take people out of the refugee camps, so that we do not encourage people to make this perilous crossing. (HC Deb, 7 September 2015b, col. 33)

The government continue to argue that since the vast majority of refugees remain within the region, this should be the area of sole focus. Yet, though stating that part of the 20,000 would be drawn from the camps and elsewhere in Turkey, Jordan and Lebanon, the government have reiterated continuously the focus on the camps alone, with the objective of the government being to 'to keep them in refugee camps rather than see them making the dangerous crossing into Europe' (HC Deb, 7 September 2015b, col. 35). This is despite the fact that up to 80 per cent of Syrian refugees are not actually housed in camps but scattered across towns in Jordan, Lebanon and Turkey, where it is difficult for the

UNHCR to reach and assist them (Macleod 17 May 2016). As such, the focus for the VPRP was to be on the camps with the priority to be on selected resettlement of individuals based on (heightened) vulnerability (Cameron HC Deb 29 January 2014, vol. 574, col. 851). For it was proposed by the House of Commons International Development Committee (2016: 19) that vulnerability within the crisis was not 'evenly spread across all refugees, and that certain groups are subject to conditions that heighten the risks they face'.

The VPRP was to operate to locate individuals at greatest risk, where evacuation from the region was the only option (May, HC Deb 29 January 2014, vol. 574, col. 889).What is more, the government position was in reaffirming that Syrian refugees were keen to stay within the region rather than accept resettlement or relocation. Tobias Ellwood (House of Commons Debate, Lebanon (Syrian Refugees), HC Deb 20 January 2015, vol. 591, col. 74), then Parliamentary Under-secretary of State for Foreign and Commonwealth Affairs, commented, on returning from Zaatari refugee camp in Jordan, that 'it is very much the case that they would like to remain in the region – as close as possible . . . as one of the largest donors to support these countries in providing refugee camps, to give them the stability they need in this hour of need'. Not only is the refugee geographically positioned external to the EU, but the government were eager to acknowledge that the Syrian refugee also wished to remain in the region.

The VPRP was significantly expanded in September 2015 due to the increased intensity of the Mediterranean crisis, with Prime Minister David Cameron confirming that Britain's acceptance of 20,000 Syrians over a five year period would fall within this programme. In 2016, the scheme was expanded to include 3,000 vulnerable children from the Middle East and North Africa, and in 2017 it expanded again to incorporate the 'most vulnerable' refugees fleeing Syria, regardless of nationality (Home Office 2019) as well as beyond the Middle East and Africa. By the end of 2018, over 11,400 Syrians had been resettled in Britain through the VPRP (Refugee Council 2019). When the resettlement programme was initially extended, Cameron (House of Commons Debate, Syria: Refugees and Counter-Terrorism, 7 September 2015b, vol. 599, col. 33) noted the significance of resettlement only for those within refugee camps. He stressed in September 2015,

> we do not believe that the right answer is for Britain to take people who have already arrived in Europe. We think that it is better to take people out of the refugee camps, so that we do not encourage people to make this perilous crossing.

This position was reaffirmed by Theresa May (2015b) at the Conservative Party conference, who noted, 'I want to offer asylum and refuge to people in parts of the world affected by conflict and oppression, rather than to those who have made it to Britain.' She went on to observe (May 2015b),

> the best way of helping the most people is not by bringing relatively small numbers of refugees to this country, but by working with the vast number who remain in the region ... While we must fulfil our moral duty to help people in desperate need, we must also have an immigration system that allows us to control who comes to our country.

A narrative was emerging that the idealised refugee was not to be found at the border of Britain, nor within the EU. Those in most need where within the camps external to the EU. Britain has been able to relocate her humanitarian support external to the EU, avoiding moral responsibility to act within the Mediterranean crisis by framing it as one of migration, which is understood legally as a national issue. The British government geographically shifted the emphasis beyond the EU, focusing specifically on the Syrian refugees in and around the region, whilst simultaneously developing a narrative of protection and humanitarianism (Abbas 2019). Indeed, Cameron (HC Debate 21 March 2016a, col. 1244) was keen to emphasise that when it came to the crisis, the focus should be 'upstream', a term employed multiple times in House of Commons debates. For instance, then Secretary of State for Foreign and Commonwealth Affairs Phillip Hammond (HC Deb, 1 June 2015, vol. 596, col. 320) insisted that 'it is essential that we respond to this crisis in depth, dealing with the causes upstream in the countries of origin'. For Hammond (HC Deb, 1 June 2015, vol. 596, col. 320), there were individuals fleeing conflict and persecution, but there were also large numbers of economic migrants that did not need protection entering into the EU illegally via traffickers; 'upstream' meant Britain could geographically provide humanitarian assistance externally to the EU, thus negating engagement and responsibility within the Mediterranean along with tackling the 'root causes' of the crisis (Greening, HC Deb, 8 February 2016, vol. 604, col. 1323).

The British response to the Mediterranean crisis was focused on securing Europe's borders; taking refugees directly from the camps and neighbouring countries but not from Europe itself; and cracking down on people-smuggling gangs. By focusing 'upstream', the camps would be the site for humanitarian aid as well as the site of the resettlement process. As Cameron (HC Deb, 7 September 2015b, vol. 599, col. 33) stressed in September 2015,

> we have taken the decision that it is better to take people from the camps. That is a good and humane decision, it will help others to be able to use those camps, and it will not encourage people to make that perilous journey.

This narrative was reinforced during the Conservative election campaign most recently in 2017, with the party manifesto stressing that the current asylum system is inefficient, being geared towards those that can make it to Britain in order to claim asylum. Instead, the Conservative government (Conservative Manifesto 2017) approach would focus on offering asylum

> to people in parts of the world affected by conflict and oppression, rather than to those who have made it to Britain. We will work to reduce asylum claims made in Britain and, as we do so, increase the number of people we help in the most troubled regions.

Emphasising the significance of providing support 'upstream', the British government is the second largest bilateral donor to the Syrian crisis since the start of the response in 2012, providing over £2.45 billion. This money went towards food rations, relief packs and vaccinations as well as medical consultations and educational requirements. In providing aid within the region, the government have co-hosted multiple international conferences such as Supporting Syria and the Region in February 2016, raising money to support Syria and her neighbours and setting goals for education and opportunities for economic growth to assist the refugees (McGuiness, 2017: 4). As well as establishing themselves as the second largest bilateral donor to the Syrian crisis, the British government has opted to define its own path in regard to the Syrian crisis, adopting a position that focuses intensively on the region. As such, governments have adopted policies of containment, distance and geographical hierarchy of need that are premised upon the vulnerability of the refugees themselves and adopt the language of 'saving lives'. Indeed, the British approach has also drawn upon what Adrian Little and Nick Vaughan-Williams (2016: 13) have identified as accompanying narratives of the 'need for enhanced border security, the targeting of traffickers and smugglers . . . and irregular migrants alike, and the invocation of emergency legislation to help [EU] member states confronted with a sudden influx of migrants'.

By setting up this narrative with the refugee camps that was founded on humanitarian principles and compassion, but also geographical isolation and containment, the government established a clear geographical distinction in need between those individuals still remaining within the region, compared with those individuals who had undertaken the journey and entered into the EU. This ultimately has led to states such as Greece and Italy bearing the brunt of the refugee crisis, with daily arrival rates skyrocketing into the tens of thousands, but it was a problem that was to be contained in Greece, Italy and Turkey, and not one that Britain needed to be engaged with – our priority was focused purely on the refugees external to the EU. For the government were taking the position that since the vast majority of refugees were still located in the region, with only 3–10 per cent having moved to Europe, the focus on resettlement was mistaken:

> If all the focus is on redistributing quotas of refugees around Europe, that will not solve the problem; it actually sends a message to people that it is a good idea to get on a boat and make that perilous journey . . . we are a humanitarian nation with a moral conscience,

we will take 20,000 Syrians. But, we want a comprehensive approach that puts money into the camps, that meets our aid commitments, that solves the problems in Syria. (Cameron, HC Deb, 9 September 2015c, vol. 599, col. 397)

This approach can be viewed as externalised humanitarian hospitality, founded on conditions in order to control, contain and exclude. Cameron developed this distant humanitarian approach further, stating

> we need a co-ordinated European response, I do not believe it should be Britain giving up our borders and joining the Schengen no-borders arrangement . . . We want to encourage people not to make that dangerous crossing in the first place, and it is worth considering this: 11 million have been pushed out of their home in Syria, and so far only perhaps 3% have made that journey to Europe, so it is important that as we act with head and heart, we help people without encouraging them to make that dangerous and potentially lethal journey. (HC Deb 7 September 2015b, col. 31)

Distant Suffering

By putting the emphasis on the camps only the government have been able to reduce the Mediterranean crisis to a Syrian crisis and focus exclusively on refugees from that region. This effectively allows the government to remove their responsibility towards other refugee crises, whilst upholding humanitarian principles. Indeed, as Theresa May herself asserted, 'wherever possible, I want to offer asylum to people in parts of the world affected by conflict and oppression, rather than to those who have made it to Britain' (May 2015b). In developing this approach, it raises interesting discussions on our understanding of distant suffering. Luc Boltanski (1999: 3) argues that suffering is socially constructed and different forms and means of suffering have come and gone over the eras. The 'spectator' who observes the suffering, as Boltanski notes, must be able to relate to, and identify with the sufferer. For they are observing the unfortunate and are not involved in the experience of the suffering and as such, may be regarded as privileged or 'lucky' people. In order to understand and respond to suffering, it needs to be recognisable. Hence there must be a general recognition with those who are suffering to 'merit political intervention based on the sentiment of pity' (Boltanski 1999: 155). As Tristen Naylor (2011: 185) comments, it is 'the act of translation-of making that which is alien known and understood' that shapes our understanding and ultimately, what makes this political. As such, there can be conflict over the identification of who the unfortunates are. Boltanksi (1999: 155) states that 'within the realm of political struggles the culture of beliefs supporting the pity corresponds to a conflict over the identification of the unfortunates whose cause is to be judged politically worthy'. Within the domain of action and the domain of representation, if you are dealing with '"excesses of unfortunates"', then who comes to the fore first?'(Boltanksi 1999: 155). In the Mediterranean crisis, the government have stressed that the unfortunates, are those external to the European Union – those residing within the camps surrounding Syria. As Boltanski (1999: 11) asserts, to arouse pity, suffering and wretched bodies must be conveyed in such a way as to affect the sensibility of those more fortunate. There has to be something to relate to and connect with in order to understand and act.

In a similar vein to Boltanski, Zygmunt Bauman (cited in Pemberton 2004: 78) writes that 'morality seems to conform to the law of optical perspective'. In developing this notion, Simon Pemberton (2004: 78) reflects how as geographical distances increase, the responsibility towards the other is diminished: 'moral indifference is inherent in the structures of industrialised society because the effects of human action far exceed an actor's moral visual capacity'. Whereas Andrew Linklater (2007) notes that the process of globalisation has made affluent societies more aware of distant suffering than ever before, but how this affects the relationship between obligations to fellow citizens and duties to the rest of humankind is unclear. However, in the Mediterranean crisis we have observed that the greater the geographical distance, the stronger the humanitarian response, leading to a narrative emerging that the 'refugee' is bound by geographical constraints in the crisis, and exists elsewhere, beyond the boundaries of the EU, leading to what Henk van Houtum (2010) refers

to as the separation of the wanted and the unwanted through logics of geography. As Boltanski (1999: 13) asserted:

> it is inherent within the politics of pity to deal with suffering from the
> standpoint of distance since it must rely upon the massification of a col-
> lection of unfortunates who are not there in person . . . For when they
> come together in person to invade the space of those more fortunate that
> they and with the desire to mix with them, to live in the same places and
> to share the same objects, then they no longer appear as unfortunates . . .

For what is in question in the European refugee crisis is precisely
the division and separation of the unfortunate and the fortunate
without which a politics of pity cannot be developed (as well as
a politics of hospitality!) (Boltanski 1999: 13).This geographical
displacement of the Mediterranean crisis and the refugee is premised upon logics of containment, exclusion and politics of externalisation that allow the British government to situate the crisis
beyond the territory of Britain and the EU, absolving themselves
of a national and regional responsibility towards the crisis unfolding within Greece, Italy or the larger Mediterranean Sea. Instead,
the focus is one of humanitarianism that engages with the refugees solely within the camps. This results in a seeming reversal
of Luc Bolstanki's distant suffering: that rather than responding
to the crisis unfolding on our geographical doorstep in the Mediterranean, the further away the suffering is, the more engaged
and active the British response appears to be. As May warned us,
'I want to offer asylum to people in parts of the world affected by
conflict and oppression, rather than to those who have made it to
Britain' (May 2015b).

In the response to the Mediterranean crisis, there has developed a logic of externalisation and exclusion that has created an
idealised refugee – a heightened vulnerable 'victim' who resides
within the regional camps. For the British governments' identification and response to the Mediterranean crisis has been muted
as they have failed to establish a connection with the individuals
suffering within the European Union, in locations such as Calais
or the camps of Greece, Italy or the Balkans. As such, persecution
is not recognised, individuals have been labelled as (economic)

migrants, which has resulted in a geographical externalisation of humanitarian aid – a hierarchy of need based on geographical locations that is founded on logics of containment, externalisation and exclusion.

Conclusion

The case study of the Mediterranean crisis is an ideal example to illustrate how hospitality, facilitated by the politics of labelling, has allowed the British state to project an externalised humanitarian hospitality. Britain has been able to present a dual image of humanitarianism and tightened refugee practices.

The chapter intertwines the theories of hospitality and labelling, as discussed in Chapters 1 and 2. It examines how the British government have successfully established a geographical hierarchy of humanitarianism, as well as established an externalisation of the refugee beyond the European Union, that is based on 'pity and compassion, but not one of justice and responsibility' (Razack 2008: 126). For the British government, the refugee does not exist within the EU. Rather the refugee is geographically positioned external to the EU, and those entering into the EU are re-labelled as (economic) migrants, thus not requiring British assistance as migration invokes national, not international law. This geographical distinction has resulted in the establishment of a hierarchy of needs, whereby the humanitarian response from Britain is not focused in the Mediterranean sea, or in the camps internal to the EU, but rather external, primarily within the camps in Lebanon, Turkey, Jordan or Syria, in a externalised projection of humanitarian hospitality. By stressing on focusing 'upstream', the British government have been able to successfully focus on distant suffering, thus containing, curtailing and upholding a humanitarian hospitality that is geographically externalised beyond Britain and the EU. For Britain, the refugee within the EU does not exist. Through drawing a demarcating line between those internal to the EU and those external to the EU, the British government have been able to establish a narrative of humanitarianism that is rooted solely in the camps in and surrounding Syria. Those who have undertaken the journey to Europe are labelled as lacking in humanitarian need, and instead are framed as part of the problem and connected to language of border enforcement, people smugglers, pull factors as well as economic immigration.

At the height of the Mediterranean crisis, David Cameron referred to refugees as 'a swarm of people coming across the Mediterranean, seeking a better life' (cited in BBC News 30 July 2015b). Now more than ever does the notion of hospitality need to be challenged and upheld. Asylum policies in Britain reveal the restrictions, as well as the hostility, directed towards the refugee figure and highlights the continued narrowing of the parameters of asylum seeking by the host. Accordingly, Derrida's approach of hostipitality helps to identify the processes of hospitality and hostility that are running parallel to one another within the British asylum process. Niklaus Steiner (cited in Bohmer and Shuman 2008: 266) notes, 'no one in Europe is arguing to have asylum abolished'; however, British governments are doing all in their power to operate a policy of diminishing numbers. The politics of hospitality and the language of labelling reveal a process where hostility is in full operation, resulting in British governments continuing to view asylum seekers as anything but refugees in need.

The final case study chapter will offer a counter-discussion to the government understanding of externalised humanitarian hospitality. Chapter 5 provides the case of local British practices of hospitality, set up by citizens in direct opposition to the British state's response to the Mediterranean crisis. The analysis presents a local practice of hospitality as resistance, offering a counter-narrative to the British government approach.

Local Practices of Hospitality

Consecutive British governments have adopted a stance towards the refugee whereby the interests of the state supersede the interests of those seeking asylum. The focus is on borders, externalisation and security of the state itself, suggesting that the politics of hostipitality, and thus hostility itself, is the overriding response to the asylum seeker. This led Gerasimos Kakoliris (2015) to ask, 'what is left of this principle of hospitality today, or ethics in general, when fences are erected at the borders, or even 'hospitality' itself is considered a crime?' This approach to hospitality reinforces the masculine state power as the source of the practice with the focus on security, suspicion, borders and protection. Yet as Mireille Rosello (2001: 10) argues, the constant referral to the power of state hospitality 'hides the fact that literal acts of hospitality are constantly going on, but at the private level'.

This chapter is an exploration of everyday practices of hospitality at the private, local level (drawing on the distinction between the public and the private sphere), examining the practices of hospitality that take place in local communities. The chapter engages with various actors such as charities and individual citizens who have undertaken practices of hospitality towards the guest, rather than the traditional focus of hospitality at the state level. In undertaking this approach to hospitality at the local level (or what can be understood as the Third Sector), this chapter is based upon thirty semi-structured interviews with individuals who engaged in practices of hospitality from mid-2015 onwards, in what has been termed the 'summer of welcome' (Simsa et al. 2018). This community response emerged due to events occurring within the European Union and the Mediterranean Sea, as well as in response to the British government's inaction at that time. In doing so, the chapter draws on the interviews to examine the practice of hospitality through two positions. First, as an internal practice of hospitality that is rooted in local community support, and second, identifying a range of external practices of hospitality that emerged, that were externalised beyond the territorial border of the state by community actors.

In examining internal practices of hospitality, it is noticeable that nearly all activities recorded were situated and organised via what can be referred to as small community groups, grassroots aid groups and local community activism. The focus of the internal practices was at the civil society level, the third sector in what Jenny Philimore, Angus McCabe, Andri Soteri-Proctor and Rebecca Taylor (2010) refer to as 'below the radar' activity. By this, they mean 'small community groups, organisations or activities that are either not registered with the Charity Commission or other regulatory body and lack a regular substantial annual income'. This is the focus of the chapter's attention, for both internal and external practices of hospitality and welcome, and offers a direct counter-discourse to previous chapters' approach to the hospitality of refugees at the state level.

Rosello (2001: 10) warns,

> because we use the same word to refer to drastically different conceptions of hospitality, voices seeking to resist the inhospitable dictates of the state often find themselves caught in double binds and contradictions that are very difficult to translate into daily tactics.

This chapter examines how community level actors have projected practices of hospitality beyond the state. The state response to the Mediterranean crisis was set out in the previous chapter, highlighting the externalisation of practices of hospitality in the quest to maintain and uphold the right to refuge, but under controlled and limited practices that retain and maintain the British control over the right to refuge and hospitality. The genuine refugee is based within the camps and urban areas in and around Syria, not the individuals who have embarked for Europe in the quest for sanctuary. Thus, what has resulted is a practice of hospitality which Judith Still (2013: 262) asserts is 'often seen as epitomising peace, breaking bread together, sharing salt. Yet, it is particularly necessary in violent times'. The chapter will end by examining hospitality as resistance against the state response to the Mediterranean crisis. The hospitality documented in these interviews is varied in its approach, but was ignited by one fact – a dissatisfaction with the hospitality provided at the state level, with many viewing their acts of personal, local hospitality as a resistance to the government approach and themselves as individuals seeking to make a difference, who said 'I can, I should'. By examining the local, community response to the Mediterranean crisis, the chapter acts as a critique of the state-centred hospitality, presenting a grassroots movement attuned to responsibility, presenting a counter-discourse, or a counter-ethics, of unconditional hospitality to the statist approach.

Local Practices of Hospitality: Trigger Events

Hospitality is a practice of inviting the other, of allowing the other to cross over a threshold from external to internal. Offering the other the mastery of one's home, without asking questions or demanding anything in return. Even with the practices of conditional hospitality, ethics is hospitality not because hospitality is what we ought to do, but rather because it is what we do, in every moment, as a way of being in relations to ourselves and others (Bulley 2017: 7). It is not just the state who is practising hospitality, but individual citizens who are capable of wielding this practice themselves.

By the summer of 2015 the Syrian conflict had escalated substantially, with neighbouring states such as Lebanon receiving over a million refugees and the country having 'the highest per capita concentration of refugees in the world' (UNHCR 2016b). The year saw an exponential increase in refugees, many with families, attempting the journey from Syria, particularly across the Aegean Sea from Turkey, seeking refuge in the European Union.

By mid 2015, refugees as a topic were beginning to hit the international press and harrowing accounts were emerging. The media documented the movement of individuals in and around the European Union, reporting on shipwrecks, drownings and mass deaths as well as conveying the images of individuals walking along newly erected borders in Hungary, seeking access to the European Union. At the same time, there was an increase in flows from the southern Mediterranean. The movement of refugees and migrants from states such as Eritrea, Sudan, Ethiopia and Somalia led to mass tragedies in the Mediterranean, whilst all the while the European Union struggled with the scale and enormity of the situation on its doorstep, instead implementing policies of border control and focusing on pull-factors (Mediterranean Migration Research Project 2016). As noted in Chapter 4, the 'crisis' has never been purely a Syrian crisis – there are multiple emergencies happening across all continents, with what should be noted as a small convergence in the Mediterranean. This is not to argue that this a global refugee crisis; far from it, as most refugees only cross one international border. But there has been a gathering of migrant trajectories within the Mediterranean that has led to a heightened situation emerging within this region. Indeed, the term refugee crisis itself is not actually referring to a crisis of refugees, but rather a political crisis over how the refugees have been handled at the European level, so in this regard, it is a crisis of the refugee, or what Alison Phipps (2019) refers to as 'reception crisis'.

By late summer 2015 there was a continuing escalation in media coverage of events within Europe, and incidents such as the suffocation of seventy-one Syrian asylum seekers in an abandoned refrigerated lorry in Austria were now making international news (Al Jazeera 27 August 2015a). Yet there was still little social or political regard for the situation within Britain. That was until 7 September 2015 when there was a sudden outpouring of grief, shock, solidarity and support, spurred specifically by social media and #RefugeesWelcome and #SolidarityforRefugees that garnered mass coverage both in Britain and abroad. This correlated with images emerging of a young child, Alan Kurdi, who had drowned when his family attempted to cross the

Aegean Sea. The images were front-page news, and sparked a massive grassroots reaction that directly challenged the British state response. Individuals felt compelled to react, and this reaction manifested in multiple ways that I will explore as hospitality. For as Heidrun Friese (2010: 327) acknowledges, hospitality 'is grounded in human sociability as well as in human vulnerability and finitude, it is not a "virtue", a sort of kindness or benevolence, but a right'.

There are multiple ways of practising hospitality, such as hospitality as an embodied practice, for 'hospitality implies a politics of comfort that applies not only to the host's and the guest's ontological security, but also to their embodied wellbeing' (Lynch et al. 2011: 15). Accordingly, this response is broken down into internal practices of hospitality, discussing the variety of responses initiated at the local level by the British public around 2015, but also external practices – practices of hospitality established by the public that extended beyond Britain.

Undertaking Local Practices of Hospitality: Spaces of Hospitality

But, what made this 'crisis' worthy of hospitality? Why was there such a response at the local, grassroots level to the events in the Mediterranean and in Europe? For there has been very little of this type of response to the ongoing war in Yemen, or even to the Somalia conflict or the Sudanese genocide, nor since with the Rohingya crisis which the UN declared was 'textbook ethnic cleansing' (BBC News 2017; UN NEWS 2017). What was it about the Mediterranean crisis that sparked this level of outpouring? Research by Amnesty International (2016) revealed that the British government's 'inhumane responses to the refugee crisis was badly out of touch with the views of their own citizens . . . they are not listening to the silent majority of welcoming citizens who take this crisis personally'. Citizens were compelled by this crisis to act en masse, creating a response rarely witnessed.

For many of the interviewees, the geographical closeness was one of the main elements in motivating their response. The 'crisis' was physically close. It was occurring in locations that were recognisable, and could be reached, with familiar locations like

Calais, Sicily, Kos and Lesvos. For Ruth Talbot (Interview 2018), trustee for the Refugees at Home charity, the geographical close-ness of the crisis was a central reason for her involvement, as there was a sense that this was unique and closer, thus increas-ing the moral dimensions of her involvement. She reflected 'the events in Europe during 2015 were so disturbing. This was hap-pening within my reach and it just seemed wrong not to try to do something'.

Andrea Hammel (Interview 2018), trustee for Aberaid, echoed the geographical location of this crisis when discussing her rea-sons for involvement in the local practices of hospitality. Hammel reflected on how the geographical closeness brought with it memo-ries of conflict within the Yugoslav wars, thus heightening her emo-tional response to the crisis. She observed,

> In some ways it seems such an overwhelming humanitarian disas-ter. And somehow, maybe I felt that, it was the shelling of Sarajevo in Dubrovnik in the Yugoslav wars – I remember having a very strong emo-tional response to that, as they were places that I had actually been to. Of course there are other wars going on outside of Europe, but they are places that I have not been to. And it could be that the Mediterranean, where I have been, I felt like it was closer – I'm slightly ashamed of that, as obviously you should feel humanitarian sympathy for all people in the world. But it could be that it was closer to home.

As Ros Ereira (Interview 2018), head of Solidarity with Refugees UK, acknowledged, the geographical significance of the crisis meant that physically, 'it felt a lot closer – we have all visited it for holidays . . . It is our holiday resort.' It was a place that we could identify and were familiar with, a privileged position in itself, but one that established a connection within this crisis. Indeed, the familiarity was the key element for many individuals responding emotionally to the crisis, as Lea Beven (Interview 2018), CEO of Calais Caravans, reflected,

> I first saw a picture on Facebook on the 31st August 2015 and it was of a guy from possibly South Sudan, and we was stood in his wellies by his shelter and it was all flooded out, and the water was up to the top of his

wellies. And I was like, where's this, and they were like that's Calais. And I said, don't be ridiculous, that is where I get my wine and they were like no really, there is a refugee camp there.

The geographical proximity was an issue shared by many interviewees, the notion that this crisis felt as if it was in our neighbourhood: 'when confronted with the issue at the local level it's very hard for people to just ignore it' (Anonymous 1 Interview 2018). As Cordelia Gohil (Interview 2018), trustee of People Not Borders stated, her involvement in the Mediterranean crisis was 'very much in response to events in 2015. There were . . . it just seemed amazing that there was this thing, almost on our doorstep', and as such she could not distance herself from it. It meant that a level of responsibility was enacted by individuals within British society with movements like Refugee Welcome and Solidarity with Refugees emerging at the grassroots level.

There were multiple reasons for involvement in hospitality during the period of 2015, and not all of it was rooted in voluntary reasons. For many interviewees, it was the opportunity to provide a skill set. For instance, as one interviewee (Anonymous 2 Interview 2018) from Cardiff noted, the crisis and the opportunities for hospitality at the local level presented multiple opportunities to strengthen their Arabic skills, and thus could help on a 'more day to day level'. Paul Hutchings (Interview 2018) was able to bring his business experience to the crisis, as was Brian Donnelly of Chorleywood4Refugees, a retired businessman. They both had the time to contribute and assist, as well as experience from their career in business. For Donnelly (Interview 2018) though, his engagement was sparked by the media imagery. He reflected 'it was that photo, a combination . . . I suppose if you are parents or a grandparent, you saw that little child and this unnecessary death and it was just one of those moments'. Whereas for others, the local response to the crisis provided a level of community involvement and friendship in what Tess Berry-Hart (2018) has termed the explosion of 'people to people' grassroots aid movements that emerged during this time.

This sentiment was expressed by Christine Nelms (Interview 2018), volunteer for Riverside Refugee Kitchen, who reflected on the overwhelming nature of events within Europe: 'I certainly struggled with that initially. You just feel . . . oh my gosh, this is so huge. If you are not careful it can totally freeze you into inaction.' Tess Berry Hart (Interview 2018) reflected on the horror of the scale and immensity of the crisis, as well as the plight of the child refugees that led to a visceral response. She reflected that

> the first child refugee I ever saw was a young eleven year old Eritrean who had come by himself via the smuggler routes – and he was so small . . . sorry . . . no, it's good . . . as people have to know . . . but, it is still feel that kind of horror that we live in a world were eleven and twelve year olds can travel by themselves, you know and live in a landfill site, rubbish heaps and you know that nobody cares. It really is quite horrifying – and that visceral reaction kept me and many people going.

Emotional reactions to the crisis factored highly as a means for involvement, yet for some, like Donnelly (Interview 2018), remaining 'emotionally detached' was a way in which to cope with the demands of the crisis and his engagement. The emotional response being too great, it was better to remain detached in order to function efficiently.

For many of the interviewees, their interaction was connected to strong feelings of government inaction in response to the refugee crisis, and the sense that individuals at the community level needed to be stepping into this humanitarian crisis that was unfolding on their doorstep. As Berry-Hart (2018) noted, there was the 'deeply held and angry feeling that governments and major INGOs were failing appallingly in helping and accommodating the vast human exodus arriving on the continent'. There was a sense that NGOs were slow to act, and that governments were 'failing to protect life and dignity' (Phipps 2019). Indeed, this was a sentiment expressed by Paul Hutchings (Interview 2018), CEO of Refugees Support Europe, who stated 'I could see the government washing their hands of it . . . particularly those in Calais, nearly every single one wanted to get to the UK, and France and the UK were colluding in quite violent ways to keep people out. I could see a complete inability and lack of willingness to engage.' As Hutchings elaborated, the government sense of inaction was a clear motivational factor for his own activism in the crisis. He reflected:

> In the summer of 2015, I was watching the news and getting very frustrated and thinking I need to get involved and do something in this mess, because, it doesn't look like anyone is, or not enough people are, or there isn't enough attention on it – you can just see suffering on a massive scale . . .

The emotional response was a strong theme within the interviewees. As Hammel (Interview 2018) reflected, it came down to a very simple fact – of assisting. She noted that 'when everything is very complicated, sometimes you don't end up doing anything. This time I was thinking, that if I can save one person, it is better than saving no one.' These sentiments were shared by Mary Evans (Interview 2018) of OASIS Hub in Cardiff, who was of the belief that 'however little help you can give it is better than nothing at all'. Lea Beven (Interview 2018) continued this thread of individual action and social responsibility. In discussing her reasons for engaging, Beven asserted,

> if nobody else is doing it, and I can provide some type of housing or accommodation, then I will, and I did. I didn't spend my time fighting, I spent my time doing . . . It didn't feel like it was . . . it was just get on with it. If nobody's going to do it, somebody's got to do it, so I might as well do it.

As Carlos Alonso-Gabizóa, volunteer for Mid-Wales Refugee Action stated, 'yeah, I wanted to do something that I would enjoy and something that wasn't for me'. Indeed the level of inaction from the government was put forward as a key reason for many of the volunteers seeking to engage and provide assistance – in the absence of a state response.

The media framing and intensification of the coverage during the summer of 2015 onwards also led many to actively engage in the crisis. Christine Nelms and Mary Evans (Interviews 2018) reflected that the imagery of the crisis was intense, provocative and emotional, highlighting starkly the human cost of the crisis.

> C: I think everyone sort of woke up a bit when that little boy was washed up on the shore. The horror of it. Sadly, they have all got used to the idea, they don't care again now.
> M: I think sadly, the problem is just overwhelming. And people can't cope with it so they switch off.

For some interviewees, the steady onslaught of (social) media on the crisis became deafening and almost impossible to ignore. However, for certain volunteers, there was no one specific point that tipped them into action regarding the Mediterranean crisis. As Hutchings (Interview 2018) described it,

> I know a lot of people were shocked by Alan Kurdi, I was shocked by that but I am not sure . . . I have heard it so many times, I am sure I was influenced by it but maybe I am post-rationalising now, I'm not sure it was the thing that did it for me. I can just remember a slow, drip, drip of people trying to cross borders, and just that sort of wave after wave of people trying to work their way towards Germany, and borders being shut. It was a steady onslaught of headlines and pictures of people, crowds of people not being respected or given the due care that they were needed.

Indeed as Hutchings developed, his response was situated in an ethical dilemma and contentment with his own life, which was in such contrast to events that he was witnessing emerging from the Mediterranean Sea. He noted (Hutchings Interview 2018): 'I was working for market research and communications for large corporate organisations, which was fine, but just thinking this is fucking pointless when there were people dying out there, which is much more serious.'

The continuous coverage of news and images was overwhelming for many interviewees, and created a harsh disconnect with their own lives that became difficult for some to ignore. One interviewee (Anonymous 1 Interview 2018) described the need to act as 'an increasing sense of guilt and obligation to help' that she connected directly with the media coverage within Europe and the Mediterranean. Mikkael Sverdov (Interview 2018) of Mid-Wales Refugee

Action Group noted the addictive media response to the crisis. Sverdov discussed the immersive and all-consuming nature of the media coverage, stating,

> it got to a point of total addiction with the news. You know, first thing in the morning I would check the news and some new atrocity happening and some other person who dehumanises everything that happens. And it comes to a point where you start questioning what is really true, and then you need to go and see for yourself in order to reconnect with the humanity of it . . . I don't think there was any one specific drop that kinda tipped. It was just . . . background noise . . . that increases and increased to a point where it is kind of deafening. And then you have to put in your own voice . . . your own noise in order to construct it somehow.

The media reportage meant that for many there was the need to bear witness themselves to these events, which the geographical closeness readily enabled. For these were familiar places, locations that seemed to be transformed by the crisis, and for many there was the need to make sense of this crisis. As Gabi Ashton (Interview 2018) from Mid-Wales Refugee Action tried to explain, she struggled to connect with the images emerging from the crisis. The media coverage was not enough and there was the need to bear witness herself to these events to fully understand and connect. She recalled 'I felt that I needed to do it. I can't really justify it, but I wanted to see for myself . . . this is what I need to do . . .'

There was also a strong religious dimension to the hospitality offered across the country, with churches across faiths mobilising in order to offer hospitality. As Reverend David Butterworth (Interview 2018) put it,

> one would hope that at the heart of any faith there is the desire and the mantra and an outworking to love your neighbour – doesn't matter where they come from or what plight they are in – try to help your neighbour in the best way that you can.

Philippa Houghton (Interview 2018) also spoke on this issue with her group 1FamilyCardiff, a refugee group set up through her local church. She declared there was a need to offer a 'welcome to other people' that emanated from her church, and the cause needed to be 'supported and justified'.

Internal Practices of Hospitality

Citizens within the UK, but also across Europe, in states such as Germany and Austria responded to the catastrophic crisis unfolding within the Mediterranean and EU areas, by enacting practices of welcome, hospitality and solidarity towards those in need in what has been termed a 'summer of welcome' (Karakayali and Kleist 2018: 232). These small below-the-radar groups, which can also be referred to as Refugee Third Sector Organisations (RTSO), are central to 'delivering small scale services at the local level, sustaining cultural identities, breaking down barriers to social cohesion and acting as advocates for marginalised communities' (Philimore et al. 2010). Lucy Mayblin and Poppy James (2018) suggested these RTSO fulfilled the demand for a (predominantly) unpopular public good (the living needs of asylum applicants), and are largely financed by the voluntary contributions of those minority of voters who favour them. RTSO might therefore, be conceptualised as gap-fillers that emerge in response to private demands for collective goods not offered by government or available via the market.

Often these RTSO were set up with individuals who had no previous experience of the refugee sector, but were motivated and moved to respond due to the events and media documentation of the Mediterranean crisis. For many, it was individuals taking the initiative to establish their own groups, whether online social media groups on Facebook or more established groups focusing on community sponsorship. As Cordelia Gohil (Interview 2018), trustee of People Not Borders, noted, there were multiple ways for the community to respond, be it through organising and managing collections, donating clothes, fundraising, establishing organisations. She reflected

> There was this explosion in my town of people going, well actually, I want to do something – let's do something. And, I could see this huge gathering of people wanting to collect – lets collect clothes, let's send

them over to Calais – that was the response. And having read over the newspapers about Calais being flooded with all these clothes that were – that people didn't need, stilettos, and items that weren't useful. Also, people well meaning but not really knowing what they were doing. Turning up over there and actually making things worse. And I had actually commented on a post that I saw on Facebook, a group that I was part of. Where everyone had been like let's collect this, let's do that, let's do something. And I commented and said, it's quite unusual for me because I don't usually get involved. Why don't we collect all the clothes and do a fundraiser and sell anything that might make a bit of money and then keep aside the things that we know will be useful from what we've collected – and only send that. And another lady who I have never met before, said that was a brilliant idea, why don't we meet up for a coffee. Which we did, and that is basically the point at which it all started to snowball.

These refugee third sector organisations (RTSO) are 'organisations of any size who specifically focus their charitable work on supporting those who have been, or are going through, the asylum system' (Mayblin 2018: 378). The groups were set up by a variety of individuals, some with experience, others with little to no background in the refugee field but who felt compelled to get involved due to witnessing events in the summer of 2015. As one interviewee noted (Anonymous 1 Interview 2018), when governments and the systems in place are unable or unwilling to offer this support, 'I think many people feel it falls to them to do something to help instead'. Ros Ereira (Interview 2018), for instance, founder of Solidarity for Refugees UK, had experience of the refugee sector, being a long-term volunteer for her local refugee organisation. She noted that when she created a Facebook event to demonstrate against government inaction at the start of September 2015, she 'honestly thought it would be like 6 friends who would be morally obliged to come stand with me in the rain, in Whitehall having a shout'. Ereira's demonstration drew over 90,000 who came out to protest the government's response to the Mediterranean crisis. The event went viral with the death of Alan Kurdi and acted as a flash point for public focus, anger, but importantly, resistance in the days after.

An issue that emerged from many of my interviewees was one of no prior knowledge of refugee politics. The crisis was their first introduction to refugee politics and policies. For Brian Donnelly, his engagement with the crisis led to the motivation to learn more. Lea Beven (Interview 2018), on the other hand, reflected on her 'ignorance' of refugee issues before her participation. She noted, '[I] had no understanding of what a refugee was – I had never heard of, or was aware of camps. I was absolutely shocked. I don't watch the news. I don't have live TV. I was very ignorant.' Similarly, Christine Nelms (Interview 2018) had no previous experience or knowledge of the refugee regime, yet she responded to a call on social media. She reflected at first that

> It was a bit of a nightmare, as it was so overwhelming . . . we had a box of shoes and we were looking where to send them and although the donations were for refugees in Calais, many of the donations were not suitable for Calais. Everything and anything. However, we were doing our best to find a suitable home for everything. So, we ended up helping a range of charities depending on what the donation was. And that is how I was introduced to OASIS . . . I thought it was great . . . and I wondered if I would fit in here. It was such a lovely environment, but so different, I'd never done anything like this before, or been in any places like this.

These third sector 'below the radar' groups are generally small, volunteer led and organised solely (or potentially limited) at the community level. Yet, Karakayali and Kleist (2016) observed within their research that those volunteers who got involved in 2015 were unique in their engagement, having little knowledge of refugee politics and who gave the 'community feeling of the voluntary work' as the primary reason for their engagement, that is, the experience of the 'summer of welcome'. As one interviewee (Anonymous 1 2018) noted of the response,

> I just wanted to help however I could to make these people's lives easier and to remind them that there were people in Europe who did care about them and would be happy to welcome them. Even if the very basic things we were providing were not truly what they needed (efficient, concrete legal support and official accommodation would have been much more useful) we felt it was important to show them that they had not been forgotten.

Indeed, Ruth Simsa et al. (2018) have referred to this reaction of the 2015 'summer of welcome' as 'spontaneous volunteers'. Spontaneous volunteers can be understood to be an 'impulsive and unplanned type of volunteering. It occurs as a response to a sudden rising crisis . . . characterized by turbulent environments and often short term increases in the number of volunteers' (Simsa et al. 2018: 105). The refugee third sector organisations during the late summer of 2015 were characterised by this phenomenon of spontaneous volunteers 'who joined impulsively because of newscasts or social media requests for help' (Simsa et al. 2018: 104). During the Mediterranean crisis, these RTSO 'exploded' within British civil society. Over 200 RTSO were established in September 2015 alone, with mobilised locals often acting in a fast and flexible manner (Berry-Hart Interview 2018). One of the key resources at the community level that they were able to employ to great effect was their 'human resource'. It became the driving force of these groups (Phillimore at al. 2010). Within the Mediterranean crisis, the political controversial nature of the refugee crisis, specifically this being a crisis of politics to respond to the refugee, led to a vacuum in state response to the crisis (Simsa et al. 2018). The vacuum of authority was filled by responders from the community, local level across Europe. As Cordelia Gohil (Interview 2018) reflected, there were numerous individuals wanting to do something in her local community: 'there was all this momentum and it wasn't going to be used in the right way. There was a danger of it just going to waste.'

There were a variety of activities involved in local, internal practices of hospitality that were recorded as of late summer 2015 onwards in response to the Mediterranean crisis. As Nick Gill (2018: 89) notes: 'a range of grass-roots organisations acted autonomously in Europe during 2014, 2015, and 2016, including delivering supplies, finding accommodation, offering medical, legal and educational support, and raising public awareness'. These ranged from organising demonstrations such as Ereira's actions, to clothes donations and clothes sorts, food collections, creating hygiene packs, or collecting other items like tents, sleeping bags, boots, winter coats, that would be arranged and organised internally, to then be sent externally. For instance the work of Aberaid, Tess Berry-Hart or Brian Donnelly fell into this category. Collecting, organising and receiving mass donations of clothes, food and items that could then be sent to offer hospitality to camps, specifically in Calais, France. Yet, the activities that emerged were not all in response to the refugee crisis as witnessed in the Mediterranean. This highlights well Gartkisch et al.'s (2017: 1841) position that RTSO have proven to be a supporting pillar to facilitate the integration, inclusion and well-being of migrants, by providing such services, improving human welfare and creating public and social values. Alison Phipps (2019) notes the 'extraordinary courage and compassion from communities [leading] with creativity, practical action and costly generosity in Calais, Lesvos and in receiving communities'. A variety of interviewees such as Christine Nelms and Mary Evans highlighted that their initial response was to the Mediterranean crisis, but their activities ended up supporting local refugee organisations. Introducing volunteers into local practices of British asylum meant volunteers witnessed not only British refugee policy externally, but also domestic asylum policy. Volunteers were able to witness the distinction in attitudes between those offered refuge through the Vulnerable Persons Resettlement Scheme, or the community sponsorship, when compared with the traditional British asylum system route where claims can take months, if not years, to resolve, with individuals barred from working, and it led to stark differences for the interviewees. As Mary Evans (Interview, 2018) noted,

> I did find it quite difficult . . . the families that were being settled in the UK had so much – all the children had iPads, their own phones, huge televisions, and I did find that difficult . . . how little others had . . . Yes, those sponsored by the government, there is such a huge difference in how they are treated compared to other refugees.

This awareness of the refugee situation beyond the Mediterranean or Syrian crises has also resulted in activities such as Refugee Connection, a befriending charity set up in London by Catherine Fleming (Interview 2018), to bring a level of individuality and humanity back to the refugee experience for those already in the British refugee system. Or Refugees at Home, a charity that recruits hosts who have a spare room, and matches them with refugees and asylum seekers who are temporarily in need of housing. It was established in October 2015 by three Jewish brothers and sisters and as Ruth Talbot (Interview 2018), trustee for Refugees at Home, reflected,

> it was born from the fact of people moving across the Med, but also because of a frustration that they were not able to do the things that they wanted to do. They had heard stories from their childhood of hosting, so they already had it in their mind that this was something that was possible.

Internal practices of hospitality then can be categorised into assisting and supporting refugees in the Mediterranean crisis directly, but also through individuals getting involved in local refugee organisations, or establishing their own organisations such as Refugees for Home to offer hospitality and welcome to refugees, beyond the Mediterranean crisis. It is through these practices that for some volunteers the awareness arose that the crisis was not simply a Syrian crisis, but a larger crisis of refuge.

Community Sponsorship

In examining internal practices of hospitality the following section will focus specifically on the Community Sponsorship programme. Community Sponsorship has provided a means by which local community groups have been able to enact and engage with practices of hospitality in what Rosello (2001) would term 'a private gesture of hospitality' that is a 'subcategory of national hospitality'. Community Sponsorship is a new programme that was developed back in October 2015, in response to the grassroots reaction to the Mediterranean crisis. The British Community Sponsorship programme is an idea that was developed from the forty-year-old Canadian private refugee sponsorship programme which has enabled robust citizenship engagement in resettlement, and which is now positioned globally as the best practice model for refugee resettlement. Due to the demonstrable success of the Canadian programme at forging 'powerful bonds between sponsors and refugees' (Global Refugee Sponsorship Initiative 2017) it is now being rolled out as part of the Global Refugee Sponsorship

Initiative to tackle the global refugee crisis (Maniatis and Bond 2018). The British Community Sponsorship programme was introduced in 2015 by then Home Secretary Theresa May (cited in *The Independent* 2015) at the Conservative Party conference. She declared:

> I know the whole country was proud of the generosity of spirit shown by the British businesses and families who offered to shelter Syrian refugees in their own properties this summer. So to help turn these acts of humanity into reality, we'll establish a register of people and organisations that can provide houses for the settlement of refugees. We'll develop a community sponsorship scheme, like those in Canada and Australia, to allow individuals, charities, faith groups, churches and businesses to support refugees directly.

Community sponsorship has allowed local communities, rather than traditionally the state, to become directly involved in the resettlement process of Syrian refugees. Communities are able to come together to submit an application and then follow through by committing to provide 'financial, emotional, and resettlement support' to help newly arrived refugees, assisting in their integration to life in their new country (Global Refugee Sponsorship Initiative 2017). Community Sponsorship in this regard offered a 'new approach to resettlement' that Amber Rudd (cited in Home Office 2017), speaking in 2017 as then Home Secretary, noted 'will help bring communities together . . . to empower and enable community groups to take on the challenging but rewarding role of welcoming and supporting a resettled family'.

Riding on the wave of the grassroots response to the events being witnessed in Europe, community sponsorship was a way for the government to tap in to this reserve of community power in order to further facilitate resettlement within the country. The focus was on the benefit of local communities and the empowering or mobilising significance of the programme. As Oliver Thomas (cited in Maniatis 2017), a community sponsor, reflected: 'I can't solve the whole Syrian crisis, but I can do something, for a few people.' George Maniatis (2017) of Open Society Foundation said of the programme, we are seeing the receiving communities themselves transformed by the experience, as powerful bonds between sponsors and refugees are established, and positive attitudes towards refugees are fostered. Sponsors frequently comment that this is the most meaningful activity they have ever been a part of.

Indeed, as Eva Jonsson (Interview 2018), ambassador for Sponsor Refugees, a charity tasked with promoting and supporting community sponsorship, stated, 'I love the sense of community. It is like bringing everyone together, it works against loneliness. It works against disenfranchisement – people thinking they can't do anything . . . yes you can!' But, she noted, it was not just a matter of empowering and supporting local communities in response to the events of the Mediterranean crisis, but the situating of the refugee family at the heart of the community, reflecting 'they [the refugees] come landing to the UK, and they will have hundreds of friends on the day they land'.

In this regard, the role of communities is central to this new resettlement programme. Supporting and prioritising communities at the heart of resettlement is in stark contrast to the traditional resettlement programme or the VPRS, where issues and shortcomings have arisen of 'refugee families isolated and struggling to adapt to their new surroundings' (Maniatis 2017). Reverend David Butterworth (Interview 2018) reflected on the first Syrian families to arrive via the VPRS to Birmingham. The families were informed 'here is your key – lock your door, close your curtains, nobody wants you here . . .'. The Home Office and regional organisations working on their behalf failed to introduce the family to local community support groups, or to provide support or information on what was present in Birmingham. The families were isolated and told to remain isolated for their own 'safety', even though this did not reflect the wishes of local communities, who wanted to extend a welcome. As Butterworth (Interview 2018) noted, this response to resettlement 'has continually, still damaged those people. They have not had what they ought to have had.' This has echoes with other VPRS programmes such as in Newtown, Powys, where it has been acknowledged that although accommodation, housing, health and educational needs have been met, 'religious and culture needs have not been met' and integration with the local community has been minimal. Megan Bowler (Interview 2018), the family support worker, noted that 'we've got nothing . . . from the get go, more talk about how community groups can help and support' was required.

Traditional approaches to resettlement and hospitality such as those documented highlight the damaging effect that community exclusion can have on resettled families, with Maniatis (2017) arguing that 'this in turn results in high rates of unemployment, depressions, stress, and other problems' further compounding the issue. Butterworth (Interview 2018) stressed that this was not how a resettlement programme should be running, especially one that purposely excluded a supportive local community. Integration and community were essential. As he noted, 'you need to be doing a lot of these things with the heart, and I think the heart got lost in this process'. Rather, it is imperative that families be placed at the heart of the community. This is where the power of the community sponsorship lies – placing refugees within an active community support structure.

In establishing a Community Sponsorship programme, the local sponsor, which must be a registered charity, has formal responsibility for the resettled family for two years and bears the costs of resettlement that is calculated at £4,500 per adult (typically £9000 for a family) (Home Office 2017). The community sponsor has the responsibility for being the direct port of contact for the family, from arrival at the airport to cultural orientation, allocating housing, accessing health and education, language training, employment and eventually becoming a self-sufficient member of the community. Community sponsors must also provide social work support, befriending, lunch clubs, fundraising for retreats and trips as well as various social gatherings, in order to strengthen and embed the resettled families within the local community. As Revd David Butterworth (Interview, 2018) noted,

we have wrapped them up with TLC but still with a business-like approach. Because in two years we need to enable them to be living and breathing British society and to be sufficiently knowledgeable in the English language, and to be getting work.

It is important to note that community sponsorship is required to provide less money and support for a shorter amount of time than the five years offered through the VPRS, local authority route. It is viewed by the government that community sponsorship should complement but not compete with the VPRS (Committee of Public Accounts 2017). Thus, the Community Sponsorship programme has a good working relationship with the Home Office, with the department being supportive and cooperative towards local groups undertaking this route, as well as with Sponsor Refugees, the designated charity for the programme. As Jonsson (Interview 2018) affirmed, although the Home Office has a strong track record for disbelief and hostility towards refugee and immigrants,

> On this matter yes, I mean there are plenty other matters which are not part of this – but, on this matter alone, they have been really, really good. If we email them, we get a response the same day, from the Home Office. And if they cannot reply, they will forward on to someone who can. And we keep meeting them, so it is a good working relationship.

Yet, part of the support to encourage local community sponsorship groups could be connected to the fact that the refugees for the community sponsorship programme are selected and screened through the same process as the Vulnerable Persons Resettlement Scheme; therefore refugees coming via both routes – Community Sponsorship and the VPRS – are included in the government's pledge to resettle 20,000 Syrians by 2020. Community Sponsorship resettled families are not viewed in addition to the government pledge (Home Office 2017). This has led to resentment at the local community level, where groups were established in order to push the target of 20,000, in the belief that establishing a Community Sponsorship group, and accepting a family, would be in addition to government figures, and not included within the pledge. As Hammel (Interview, 2018) reflected on the Aberaid case,

> I think practically, I mean for me, it was if we can just push the government, if they are willing to bring in 20,000, can we just push them a few more and then maybe we can bring in more, a way to circumnavigate this restrictive government response.

Community Sponsorship had been viewed as a way to resist the restrictive government pledge of 20,000 over five years. Community Sponsorship was seen as a way for communities to maximise hospitality within the crisis:

> it did come as a little bit of a shock that the family that we actually were helping to resettle in Aberystwyth actually counts towards the 20,000 . . . it is completely, and utterly, it is a scandal . . . Because I am thinking that it is a privatisation of what should be a public task – to provide sanctuary, or providing refuge, providing asylum. It is a government sanction, it is not something in this structure of the state, at the moment that private individuals should do. (Hammel Interview 2018)

Indeed, Jonsson (Interview 2018) of Sponsor Refugees confirmed that 'we as a group are not happy to be included in the national level. We accept it for the now to see how it works but we are trying to get additionality.' The issue of additionality was eventually addressed in June 2019, when Sponsor Refugees were successful after a year long campaign to have Community Sponsorship numbers added on top of VPRS numbers. They argued

> this is something we have been calling for and is crucial since all the work of planning resettlement, fundraising and welcoming families is done by the community in this case, so shouldn't be included in the Government run figures for resettlement.

Indeed, alongside the issue of additionality being rectified, the government noted that the 20,000 pledge by 2020 was being extended by one year to 2021, with the government committing to accept a further 5,000 refugees as part of the New Global Scheme which unites the Vulnerable Persons Resettlement Scheme and the Vulnerable Children's Resettlement Scheme. As of 2019, the government have accepted 15,997 refugee through VPRS, 1,410 through VCRS and 281 refugees have been welcomed as part of the Community Sponsorship programme (Citizens UK 2019; Sponsors Refugees 2019).

Yet, this question of additionality has allowed for further questions to be raised regarding the accessibility of the community sponsorship. For instance, the accessibility and knowledge required in order to establish a Community Sponsorship group is extensive. Hammel (Interview 2018) noted that Aberaid has a high proportion of academic and intellectual individuals, 'with years worth of funding and application writing experience, yet it is still quite hard . . . it is a difficult process'. Whereas Butterworth (Interview 2018) reflected on the knowledge required of local civic affairs required for the application, and the need to know who is in what position where, in order to sign off and have approved a variety of issues connected with Community Sponsorship. As he noted,

> you have to work hard to get through it all – you can not be willy-nilly. You need the senior people in the area to sign things off, but you then need to know who they are – it's knowledge! [. . .] You need the confidence that education offers to tackle community sponsorship. I think it would have put a lot of people off this, because in the beginning the Home Office made it out as if anybody could do this. And then they changed that you need to have charity status – so that precludes a lot of people . . . If you are not knowledgeable in civic and local affairs it could be very hard . . .

Furthermore, Community Sponsorship, as connected to the VPRS, has meant that Community Sponsorship has remained focused solely on Syrian refugees, overshadowing refugees fleeing other countries, which Nick Gill (2018) has referred to as the suppression of welcome. Whilst the VPRS has expanded to include other nationalities of refugees, beyond Syrians, this has not crossed over to the Community Sponsorship programme. By solely focusing on Syria, Community Sponsorship has 'came to overshadow refugees fleeing other counties and situations, as well as the many millions of internally displaced people that did not or could not cross an international border and therefore did not qualify as refugees'. As Gill (2018: 89) elaborated,

> the [British] government refusal to assist in the EU/UNHCR Quota System and their instance of working only 'upstream' meant that the British government response reinforced the Syrian (or at least the regional) only crisis, by refusing to assist other nations involved within the Mediterranean crisis.

Reece Jones (2016) has called it a constrained approach that limited the 'temporal and geographical scope'. A response that 'legitimized refugees from Syria while other migrations, classified as economic or voluntary migrants are represented as taking advantage of the Syrian refugee situation to sneak into Europe'. Thus, the community sponsorship programme 'is not above reproach' (Gill 2018: 89). For local refugee activists keen to be involved in practices of hospitality, it has meant that their welcome has been limited only to Syrians, despite the variety of nationalities involved in the Mediterranean Sea. This has resulted in the local practices of hospitality enacted through community sponsorship being severely limited, or conditioned towards a specific guest only – the Syrians. Accordingly, Nick Gill (2016: 159) argues that activism in pursuit of compassion is distinctive because it is often carried out in full view of the existing authorities (rather than surreptitiously) and it tends to accept the existing configurations of power that bureaucrats are at liberty to exercise. Activism in pursuit of functionaries often entails a degree of capitulation to existing configurations of power that may be unpalatable to activist groups. The community sponsorship programme has allowed the government to retain a highly conditional hospitality of refugees accepting only Syrian refugees that are vetted through the UNHCR, arguing against additionality to the 20,000 and having communities bear the financial and emotional responsibility of assisting the government in meeting the 20,000 pledge.

External Practices of Hospitality

Within the community response approach to the refugee crisis was the local community reaction to offer hospitality, but not just at the local, national level. What was interesting about the response from a variety of community responders was the externalisation of hospitality practices that reached beyond the confines of the British state. Hospitality was projected beyond, into other geographies and territories, as a means for individuals to collectively respond as effectively as they saw fit to the refugee crisis. The result of this external practices of hospitality saw British citizens offering hospitality in camps in France such as Calais or Dunkirk, offering support on Italian isles such as Lampedusa, in camps in and around Greek isles, such as Lesvos or Samos; or providing aid along transit routes such as in Macedonia or Hungary. As Elisa Sandri (2017: 66) notes:

> Volunteers brought humanitarian aid close to their home, reaching the informal refugee camps just by crossing the English Channel, travelling within France, or from other European Countries. The proximity and informality of the camp allowed for an occasional participation in humanitarian aid work, as volunteers could commit to this work flexibly.

In this aspect, hospitality is able to become a spatial practice, as argued by Bulley (2017), and it was citizens, individuals or collectives working together through the establishment of RTSO that enabled this externalised hospitality.

The external practice of hospitality, rather like the internal hospitality, was characterised by some of the same traits. As Berry-Hart (2018) noted, it was 'fast, effective, often chaotic and prone of course to the usual dangers of fraud, unreliable management and chaotic communications'. As Berry-Hart (Interview 2018) admitted, 'there were stories of people going over to Calais and just dumping stuff – high heeled shoes and wedding dresses, and all sorts of ludicrous things'. Yet, at the same time, the chaotic approach was 'also immediate, flexible, and targeted on specific needs' (Berry-Hart Interview 2018). As Simas et al. (2018: 110) acknowledge, spontaneous volunteers, those who travelled abroad to assist in the crisis, were invaluable:

> due to insufficient official response, the role of spontaneous volunteers was crucial: In many situations, spontaneous volunteers substituted for governmental and civil society actors. Spontaneous volunteers were often the first responders at the scenes, and worked before civil society organisations or government bodies took over.

Emphasis has also been placed on the spontaneous voluntary actions as a collective network of support, bringing people together (Clegg Interview 2018). Indeed, Darragh McGee and Juliete

Pelham (2018: 27) observed, 'the informality which marks their distinct "grassroots" form of humanitarianism served as a striking alternative to the state humanitarianism which is said to have proliferated under neoliberal regimes'. The benefit of this style of hospitality meant that grassroots groups were able to benefit from their immediate and flexible position, whereas aid agencies or large international organisations faced multiple restrictions via local government policies or funding restrictions which affected their ability to work effectively and efficiently on the ground. These restrictions did not apply to small refugee groups set up to respond, so that 'a shelter that could take six months to sign-off by an INGO could be built in an afternoon by grassroots' (Berry-Hart 2018). A vast, active response emerged within the vacuum of inefficient government and aid agency inaction. Within the void of state inaction, 'unencumbered by state bureaucracies', the grassroots groups 'operated under a self-ascribed authority derived largely from their own moral insistence of the human rights to a dignified threshold of life' (McGee and Pelham 2018). For Frances Webber (cited in Fekete 2018), the people involved within the refugee crisis were an 'army of crowd-funded and self-funded volunteers which provided genuine care rooted in humanitarian principles rather than security concerns'. She argued that 'it's precisely because the EU is so determined not to allow what it calls "spontaneous migration" – what anyone else would recognise as "refugees needing help" – that they are prepared to do what is morally unjustifiable'.

Many of the interviewees involved in external hospitality noted the lack of state or large aid agency response, and for many, this was a double incentive to be reacting to the crisis, as the state absence was so apparent. Carlos Alonso-Gabizóa (Interview 2018), of Mid-Wales Refugee Action, first visited the Calais camp in the winter of 2016. He reflected on his first trip as 'very intense. It was very positive, very sad. You saw the best in humanity and the worst in humanity . . . it hit hard.' He went on further though, referring to the lack of a state response within the camps, what Sandri (2017: 70) refers to as 'institutional abandonment and intentional indifference . . . violence inaction . . .'. Alonso-Gabizóa (Interview 2018) noted that due to the vacuum of state responsibility and aid actually it was incredibly empowering. He recalled

I went there and it was very empowering to see the state basically doesn't give a shit . . . and then seeing a bunch of volunteers providing what the state doesn't provide. With no resources, people are able to find a way to sort and to provide the minimum for people. And coming from a humanitarian position – you know, we can do these things ourselves. So, doing these things was very empowering. Very sad, but I was very happy of my involvement.

Indeed, Calais was distinct in this instance, as it never received official refugee camp status or legal approval, unlike other camps around the world. The absence of international humanitarian agencies led the director of Médecins Sans Frontières, Vicki Hawkins (cited in Sandri 2017: 65), one of the few agencies allowed to enter into the Calais Jungle, to refer to the refugee camp as 'the worst I have seen in twenty years of humanitarian work'.

Other volunteers noted the chaotic approach to the crisis and the potential inefficiency of other individuals working alone, taking items to Calais, or the variety of grassroot actors or agencies, and started to question their purpose. As Sandri (2017: 74) observed, due to the volunteers having no experience or training in humanitarian work, the aid provided was 'impromptu, tentatively trying to find solutions for the ever-evolving situation in the camp'. As such the externalisation of hospitality as witnessed in response to the refugee crisis meant that the practices of hospitality were unknown, with the exchanges and interactions between the host and the guest resulting in 'one party second guessing the other's desire or needs'. And this unknown element of the external hospitality, for many, created 'moments of malaise and discomfort, as well as moments of pleasure and joy' (Rosello 2001: 171).

Indeed, volunteers faced systemic pressures and structures from the EU. For instance, the lack of official recognition of refugee camps as spaces of humanitarian concern, the continuation of hard borders and the focus of the EU on the crisis, as one solely of Syrian refugees. As Alexander Betts and Paul Collier (2017: 93) noted, 'while the refugee issue has dominated the EU agenda, it's content was all about Europe rather than about refugees'. As Syd Bolton (cited in Fekete 2018) highlights, the joy of humanitarianism has been tempered by the tensions and barriers manoeuvred by the EU, whereby 'we've seen human rights defenders in Lesvos facing huge fines of tens of thousands of Euros, simply for providing refuge for people rescued on the coast'. Martina Tazzioli (cited in Fekete 2018) argues that by establishing and maintaining barriers, 'I was wondering whether the EU is attempting to create a division between the 'good humanitarians' – larger institutions that are integrated into the system – and other smaller organisations, that are local and independent.'

Yet, this same 'impromtuness' and flexibility did lead to tensions arising within volunteers regarding best practice. As Paul Hutchings (Interview 2018), CEO of Refugee Support Europe, reflected on his experience in Calais back in 2015 and 2106, there were 'lots of conflicts and I started to question whether it was the best use of my time'. Indeed, Lea Beven (Interview 2018) noted that her own group splintered due to disagreements over moral and ethical engagement with the refugees. Beven created the group originally to take caravans over to Calais to provide basic shelter and safe sleeping conditions, particularly for children and the youth. She reflected that 'I could offer safety, and it was coming to the end of summer and I was like, "oh my god, it's going to be winter, what are they going to do?"' Yet, she reflected on the tensions she faced, observing,

It was really interesting because there are lots of politics. For instance, lots of volunteers wanted to have their pictures taken with refugees, handing over the caravan that they had fundraised for, which I thought was a very uncomfortable thing to do.

She continued:

It's all very nice taking a caravan to a group of people who really need it but you've got to remind yourself how it feels for that person being handed the caravan and you know, and if you stand next to them and say, I know you've got greasy hair and dirty knickers but can we have a picture with you . . . it's not right . . . They don't really have a choice, so it felt really sad that so many volunteers needed the photo side of things. So, we splintered into a smaller group of people who were not interested in being a hero – we were not there to be heroes – we just wanted to be there to support people who needed supporting . . . dignity – that is it.

Indeed, Hutchings (Interview 2018) was critically reflective of the grassroots movement that offered external practices of hospitality, aware of the flaws and limitations of the act of volunteering – the chaotic and spontaneous characteristics, and the need for a more rigorous approach. He noted,

> [I] was very uncomfortable to begin with . . . I think what a lot of the volunteer sector is crying out for is someone with a business approach to it . . . it's not all about, trying to say "there, there" or give out blankets . . . it's someone who is a bit more rigorous around . . . you know this stuff all needs to be paid for, and we need to get the resources in place, we need to be a bit strategic about our communications. So although it was running a volunteer operation in the humanitarian sector and seems like a big departure [from previous work], I had been running a business . . . it's not quite a big leap.

As Sandri (2017) reflected in this new form of humanitarianism, it can 'be interpreted as a sense of moral fulfilment that provides comfort and satisfaction to one's own self reducing the issue to an often narcissistic self-reflection'. This was an observation noted by Lisa Malkki (2015), who observed that within the humanitarian community, 'there is an undeniable neediness' from those involved in humanitarianism, and this sense of personal satisfaction, or validation, was present for some within the refugee crisis, highlighting an intriguing element to the process of externalised hospitality. Indeed, these were sentiments that were raised by a few of my interviewees; Paul Hutchings (Interview, 2018), for example, reflected that his engagement in the crisis was founded on 'the need not to have regrets later on in life'. Certainly, the volunteer movement within the crisis has been faced with criticism, that 'humanitarian actors have been cast as naive, or as "white saviours" or overly charitable in intent; as diminishing refugee agency or as ineffective' (Phipps 2019). Whereas Gabi Ashton (Interview 2018) of Mid-Wales Refugee Action and Moira Vincentelli (Interview, 2017) of Aberaid both referred to the need to bear witness in order to understand. As Ashton reflected,

> I was intrigued I think . . . and curious to know what it would be like to experience. And then I thought I would understand, for reading the newspaper and hearing on the media, I couldn't connect with it. I

needed to meet people face-to-face. Human to human and be alongside them to understand the situation . . . So, it's probably quite selfish. You know what I mean, it was for me . . . and I couldn't . . . I needed to be there in the situation rather than from a distance.

Hospitality as Resistance

In concluding this chapter, the following section will engage with the practice of hospitality, be it internal or external, and viewing this practice as a hospitality of resistance. In discussing hospitality as resistance, I draw inspiration from Rosello (2001: 61), who reminds us, 'sometimes, hospitality is a dissident option, the choice of one individual, who may not be able to impose his or her convictions for very long but can still make a difference'. For many of the volunteers I engaged with, their response to the refugee crisis was rooted in resistance to the British government inaction and inadequacy, as well as anger over the continued plight of the refugees, in what Moira Vincentelli (Interview 2017) referred to as the 'incomprehensible response'. Hammel (Interview 2018) reflected on her stance and engagement, noting,

> I did feel that the British response was totally inadequate – this is such a large country, they could have taken in many more. On the other hand, you have Germany taking in up to a million – which has raised its own problems, as they couldn't really handle it – issues with accommodation, social work and all that. So I see both sides. When everything is very complicated, sometimes you don't end up doing anything. This time I was thinking, that if I can save one person, it is better than saving no one. That might have had something to do with it.

Rosello reminds us that acts of hospitality that appear peaceful, or community led and sociable, can actually disguise deeper issues of hospitality that operate through resistance, or dissident actions. She clarifies (2001: 174),

> if perfectly peaceful moments of shared hospitality sometimes hide ugly structures of larger inhospitality, they also coexist with other dissident hospitality. Hospitality then goes underground, becomes a form of resistance where a subject deliberately chooses to occupy the position of host that the system denied him or her.

Hospitality, Rosello (2001) warns us, is a challenging practice, both for the host and the guest, that will shake both to the core, an experience highlighted by Ruth Talbot (Interview 2018). She spoke of her frustration and motivation due to the government response, noting,

> I was very frustrated by the way that the people who were in those camps were portrayed as somehow choosing this . . . and I kept thinking, nobody would choose this, there must be more to this . . . so it was partly, I can do something, and I should do something.

As noted within the first chapter on hospitality, risk is a central factor for hospitality, regardless if its conditional or unconditional, hence why Derrida (1999b: 70) acknowledged that it was 'unbearable'. Rosello (2001: 176) argues that those engaging with hospitality, be it the state or individual practices, must be willing to test themselves and their potential willingness to live with the fear of hospitality,

> [for] if the guest and the host are not willing to take that risk and do not welcome the possibility of being challenged, shaken, changed by the encounter, then there is no hospitality either . . . it constantly tests the host's and the guest's thresholds of fear, and their willingness to live with that fear, and with their malaise.

Many of the interviewees perceived their actions as a means of resistance, of defying and making a stand against the British government. For Talbot (Interview 2018), activism as resistance was central to her actions:

> It is not just a case of 'I can' [do something] but actually in doing this, I am challenging that . . . this is my . . . I am in my 60s and my children are grown up and I say to them, this is my activism . . . this is me rebelling against the prevailing narrative. This is me refusing to accept you know stuff. I just refuse it.

Indeed, this was a position acknowledged by Mayer (2018: 238), who through her work highlighted that 'the great majority of the volunteers see their engagement not only as a way to provide support for refugees, but also to oppose migrants' social exclusion and marginalisation'. Mayer found through their research that over 90 per cent of the volunteers who were involved in the refugee crisis perceived their engagement as a larger statement on racism and xenophobic tendencies. Indeed, Elisa Sandri (2017: 66) argues that external practices of hospitality in the refugee camps can be characterised as resistance, for

> grassroots organisations at this particular border carried out humanitarian work while bringing to the fore the violence of the state and border regimes practices. Volunteer humanitarians in Calais created a form of civil disobedience that was not informed by unified political views but by the lived experience of volunteers in the camp.

In an extract from the Mid-Wales Refugee Action group, the members reflected on the lack of humanity witnessed at the state level, across Europe:

> Alonso-Gabizóa (Interview 2018): There is a great lack of humanity . . . and its not just the British government . . . it's in the EU in general. It's . . . and the attitude is hostile . . . the hostile environment defines so much . . .
>
> Ashton (Interview 2018): People not taking responsibility, or denial of responsibility . . .
>
> Lalor (Interview 2018): I think we are being quite mild about it . . . it's brutal, it's really absolute brutality . . . I think people just don't realise.

Yet, the resistance was not simply at the external practices of hospitality, but also directed at internal practices of hospitality in Britain itself, with activism targeting the current asylum policies, particularly the hostile environment. Aliya Khan (Interview 2018), a solicitor for Hope Projects, argued that her organisation was created directly as a resistance against the hostile environment and the overt denial of humanity afforded to refugees. Whereas Waging Peace, a human rights organisation which campaigns against genocide in Sudan and supports Sudanese refugees within Britain, experienced an overwhelming increase in volunteers interested in supporting the organisation during the 'summer of welcome' as a way to respond, act and engage in refugee politics (Crawther Interview 2018). This position on large narratives of prejudice, racism, xenophobia or intolerance was highlighted multiple times throughout my interviews. One interviewee (Anonymous 1 Interview 2018) expressed that she felt anger, guilt and sadness at the government response, and the need 'to demonstrate that the government's views did not represent my own, and also that unless we did something to help, nothing was actually going to be done to support those in need'.

Colin Harvey (2000) notes that within Britain, refugees have been a common and important site for resistance, but even within the Mediterranean crisis, as Aliya Khan (Interview 2018) noted, 'the response to the crisis was varied. There was a lot of sympathy, but not empathy.' Activism and resistance as a stand against the government approach were not common reactions, but were well documented within the primary research and became a means for volunteers to spur themselves on. For many volunteers, perception was that their actions were deliberately provocative towards the British government. As Christine Nelms (Interview 2018) noted of her actions and engagement in the crisis, 'we were pretty disgusted at the British response (and the response throughout Europe) . . . We think of ourselves as the resistance'. Reverend Butterworth (Interview 2018) asserted that his actions were deliberately provocative towards the government, 'from the get-go'. As Butterworth argued, his stance in welcoming and offering hospitality within Britain 'was to challenge the government . . . [I'm] not afraid of challenging the government. The government do not have the power . . .' The overriding need for a welcome and place of sanctuary being the driving force to tackle the government has seen community members operating as a form of resistance to state sanctioned hostipitality.

Conclusion

The summer of 2015 exposed a deficit in state responsibility to respond efficiently, humanely and effectively to a crisis on the doorstep. As British governments developed an externalised hospitality that centred the crisis, in and around the Syrian conflict solely, the community approach was contradictory. Rather than perpetuating policies of containment and control, a politics of welcome and solidarity emerged across Europe, particularly in Britain, where individuals developed an emotional response to the unfolding crisis. Indeed, as Alison Phipps (2019) notes, a 'movement has developed of people of conscience working as allies in various points of both acute need and reception'. Individuals were mobilised to respond to a crisis that felt closer to home, and despite the rise of xenophobia and far-right extremism that have countered the 'summer of welcome' (Phipps 2019), the interviews reflected an engaged, proactive, flexible community orientated response that operated at the internal and external level, and adopted a variety of methods in which to respond to the refugee crisis.

Chapter 5 has explored the various ways in which practices of hospitality operated at the community level, in response to events in the Mediterranean in 2015 onwards. Through examining practices of internal and external hospitality, the chapter examined how sub-state actors have utilised and employed hospitality and projected it beyond the confines of the state, as well as examining some of the various ways in which this hospitality has manifested. To reiterate the views of one interviewee (Anonymous 1 Interview 2018), the assistance might have failed to offer what was truly needed, namely 'efficient, concrete legal support and official accommodation', but the support offered was grounded in a politics of hospitality and welcome, to 'show them that they had not been forgotten'. The chapter ends with an examination of hospitality as resistance, to highlight the various ways that individuals engaged with hospitality, and saw it as a means of active resistance against the hostile politics of the government. What is highlighted is an extreme dissatisfaction with the hospitality provided at the state level, and compulsion by many that 'I can, I should'.

Thus, this chapter is a celebration of individual and collective agency in the face of a crisis, as well as the rejection of hostile practices. The traditional perception of hospitality is one of a (masculine) sovereign power relation 'based on the sovereign possession of the home and its space' towards the guest (Derrida cited in Bulley 2017: 13). It is an unequal power relation between state and guest. The assumption is of the state as the locus of hospitality. Yet, as Dan Bulley reflected, the movement towards an ethics of post-sovereignty is one of not assuming state-centrality, but examining the 'habitus of experience, where ethical practices are part of everyday, ongoing encounters . . .'. Within the twenty-first century, hospitality is positioned at the epicentre of our political, social and economic life for refugees, asylum seekers, immigrants – a hospitality that is wielded aggressively by states such as Britain, who wrap the practice up in externalised humanitarian ideals whilst focusing specifically on containment, prevention and deterrents. Whereas, what the previous analysis highlights is that there is an ethical counter-discourse of hospitality at play that has emerged from the community level. One where local citizens have said 'I can' and resisted the state-centric, confined approach of hospitality. Furthermore, the community level response has also seen the practice of hospitality projected by citizens beyond the confines of the state, in a growing network of hospitality practices that support, welcome and offer solidarity to refugees in the absence of state support. The chapter highlights that hospitality is not a static, state-centred practice. Rather it is flexible, adaptive, fast and can be wielded by an array of non-state actors in a humanitarian and ethical approach, both internally and externally to the state.

The 'Christmas Invasion'?

Christmas Day 2018 broke to the news that five boats with forty individuals had been intercepted while attempting to cross the English Channel – one of the busiest shipping lanes in the world. At its narrowest, the English Channel crossing is only twenty miles, from the coast of France to the coast of England, but British identity and British refugee policy is grounded in the notion of the 'spatial separation of an island, psychologically distant' from Europe, and continental refugee concerns (Daddow 2013: 212–13). Despite state aspirations of isolation, 25 December 2018 saw boats arriving on the shore of Deal, in Kent, and the boats being intercepted by local RNLI and coastguard crews. Furthermore, media reports were emerging of more seizures of boats by French crews in French waters. The individuals making these crossings, which included unaccompanied children, were Afghans, Iranians, Iraqis and Kurds by nationality, and were looking to apply for asylum in Britain (Townshead 2019).

However, the British response to these landings was one of security, prevention and curtailment, whereby humanitarian concerns were marginalised and state interests dominated. In the days that followed, Home Secretary Sajid Javid relocated two Border Force vessels to patrol the English Channel crossing, as the duty of care was to the British border (Home Office 2018). In similar fashion to his approach to the Mediterranean crisis, Javid referenced the need to work 'upstream' (see Chapter 4). By focusing 'upstream' the government would be able to prevent migrants from undertaking the dangerous journey – which was the key priority – to not have refugees claim asylum at British borders, a principle embedded in the Conservative Manifesto (2017). Javid declared in the aftermath that he had a 'duty of care to protect human life'. He spoke of the dangers of crossing the busiest shipping lanes and highlighted the risk to life, particularly the lives of young children undertaking the journey. Yet, simultaneously, Javid questioned the motives of the individuals and asked why they were making the hazardous journey to Britain, when France was already a safe country. Indeed, he (inaccurately) stressed that 'the widely accepted international principle' is that those seeking asylum should claim it in the first safe country that they reach – be that France or elsewhere. Javid then went on to challenge the genuineness of the individuals seeking refuge, undermining their credibility, and argued that 'economic migrants' should not be allowed to settle illegally in Britain this way (BBC 2019). He noted that

> People should not be taking this very dangerous journey and, if they do, we also need to send a very strong message that you won't succeed . . . You are coming from France, which is a safe country. In almost every case you are claiming asylum in the UK but if you were a real, genuine asylum seeker then you could have done that in another safe country. (BBC 2019)

For Javid and the British government, these individuals crossing the English Channel were not genuine refugees, for someone genuinely in need of sanctuary would have claimed asylum immediately elsewhere. This reductionist approach to refuge, however, overlooks the multifaceted myriad of factors, such as existing kinships and family connections, that were compelling individuals to apply for asylum in Britain (Refugee Council 2018).

These Christmas arrivals however, were not the first to cross the English Channel that month. Indeed, these vessels joined a plethora of 539 'migrants' (Home Office 2018) who had attempted cross the English Channel over the months of November and December 2018 via a variety of boats, inflatables and assorted craft, with over 40 per cent having been 'successfully' intercepted by French coastguard (BBC 2018). In responding to the Channel crossings, Javid declared the situation a 'major incident', despite its size (Home Office 2019), and the Home Office identified connections between the crossing and organised criminal gangs smuggling illegal immigrants (BBC 2018). The December Channel crossing incident is another key example of what has been examined within this book – of the practice of hospitality and the core conditional hostility that resides within it, whereby state security and protection trumps the sanctity of refuge. Facilitated by the politics of labelling, we see that as the refugee travels over the English Channel crossing with the intention to apply for asylum, they are instead re-labelled by the British government into illegal immigrants. They are transformed into something other, something dangerous. If they were genuine refugees, it was reasoned, they would not have travelled, certainly not to Britain. Importantly, in response to the Channel Crossing events, Javid stressed that British refugee policy

> clearly states that if an individual travels through a safe third country and fails to claim asylum, it will be taken into account in assessing the credibility of their claim. Following these recent events, I have instructed my officials to look at how we can tighten this further and ensure these provisions are working effectively. (Home Office 2019b)

Javid was projecting humanitarian hospitality beyond the shores of Britain, stressing first, that asylum should have been applied for in previous states traversed, such as France, and second, that hospitality would not be granted at the border of Britain. Again, there was the re-emphasis by Javid of the significance of Britain focusing 'upstream', in order to halt the movement of individuals (Home Office 2018), and a redoubling of the position that refugees would not be welcome at the border. He was also reaffirming the myth that refugees needed to seek protection in the first safe country – a requirement that is not asked of the refugee in the 1951 Refugee Convention. Through labelling, Javid was able to alter the approach to the incident, whilst stressing the humanitarian concerns and the plight of undertaking such a crossing; the individuals were re-labelled as illegal immigrants, with language of criminal gangs and smuggling connected to the incident, and the overall credibility of their claims undermined. Yet, as Maurice Wren, head of the Refugee Council (cited in Refugee Council 2018) countered, 'the fact that people are boarding flimsy boats to cross one of the world's busiest and most dangerous shipping lanes highlights the sense of fear and hopelessness that is gripping so many of the people stuck in Northern France'.

Wood (1985) argues that labelling is used in the ranking of people according to moral proximities. But, in regard to the Mediterranean crisis, and this particular Channel crossing incident, we are witnessing the reversal of hierarchical labelling towards the refugee other, based on geographical closeness to Britain. As such, those who are geographically closer to Britain, and situated within the EU, are labelled as migrants, and thus not enacting British state responsibility. By fracturing and privileging the limited label of refugee, as Javid did, the British government have established whether they are actually seeking refugee status or not, as economic migrants are 'undeserving of help or sympathy' (Jones 2016). British refugee policy has attested that the genuine refugee resides within the camps and regions surrounding Syria, geographically external to the EU –the refugee is geographically positioned further away through the politics of labelling. Through labelling, and intertwined with hospitality, the power of the labeller and the politics of labelling are on full show. Refugees were seeking sanctuary and refuge within Britain, but the successful practice of hospitality, facilitated by the politics of labelling, has been able to sustain the state approach of security, control and reduction. The framework of hospitality and labelling can be witnessed in practice, and successfully protects British state interests regarding responsibilities to refugees.

A New Approach to Hospitality

The aim of this book has been the examination of the role and figure of the refugee as situated in British refugee policy, examining the denial and transference of responsibility, as well as the wielding of humanitarian protection as a state practice. The book has adopted a two pronged approach to the British refugee system, introducing and examining first, the theoretical frameworks of hospitality and labelling, before then applying the frameworks to three case studies: the British internal asylum system, the British response to the Mediterranean crisis, and the counter-narrative case study of local community practices of hospitality.

Through linking hospitality and labelling, the book presents innovative new ways of examining refugee policies, allowing deeper insights into the notions of power, identification, responsibility, language and externalisation within the British refugee system. Dallal Stevens (1999b: 32) argued that the current British asylum system has not perceived humanitarian protection as a priority, as compared to heightened border practice and deterrence. The argument developed in this book is that actually the state has wielded the practice of humanitarianism as a means to uphold those same restrictive practices towards the refugee of deterrence, curtailment, containment and management. Humanitarianism, throughout the practice of hospitality, has been co-opted as a facade for preventing refugees accessing their right to asylum. Through the facilitation of labelling in particular, the British state has been able to transform the refugee figure into alternative, fractured labels that then negates the government's responsibility to assist. Instead of being a refuge, the British state becomes a fortress.

Chapter 1 introduced the concept of hospitality, and the traditional, state-focused approach of engaging with this theoretical concept. Hospitality simply can be understood as the right of the stranger, be it the refugee other, to arrive at a territory and not be treated with hostility. Hospitality is about how we position and engage with the other when they enter into our midst, the fear that arises from the openness of unconditional hospitality and xenophobia towards the 'parasitical' guest when states try to protect the practice of hospitality from abuse of the undeserving guest. The chapter sought to develop the theory and construct an approach to hospitality whereby, framed by humanitarian considerations, hospitality is projected externally from the state. Through humanitarian hospitality, the chapter argued that a facade of aid is developed that obscures the practices of containment, control and deterrence that are employed. A select few can be offered welcome, thus highlighting the practice, but the welcome is founded upon a hierarchy of suffering employed by the state, with only the most vulnerable given access. The majority are deemed as parasitical, to be controlled, regulated and curtailed. Chapter 2 then introduced the framework of labelling, examining the various ways of approaching labelling, particularly though the work of Zetter, Becker and Foucault, to highlight the framing and significance of labelling. The chapter then went on to examine the politics of labelling, the framing of the other, as well as analysing the significance of the labeller in the politics of labelling. Labels do not emerge within a political vacuum – as we saw, they are inherently political. Therefore, it is crucial to examine how states label specific groups, such as refugees, as a way to examine their international responsibilities. For words matter, labels matter, and how we label a group such as refugees or migrants is saturated with power, conferring access to rights and responsibilities, so that the fracturing of a label is the fracturing of a right.

Chapters 3–5 presented three case studies where the theoretical framework of the practice of hospitality, facilitated by the politics of labelling, were then examined. Chapter 3's case study was a contemporary historical empirical examination of the construction of the idealised genuine refugee in consecutive governments refugee politics. The chapter identified that (negative) responses to the refugee as well as the adoption of stringent refugee policies are nonpartisan. The case study drew on extensive archival research from Hansard, and analysed, over a thirty-year period, the creation of an idealised refugee, where consecutive British government have been able to uphold the practice of hospitality and refuge while simultaneously making the practice of refuge unattainable. Hospitality and labelling operate within the system, by establishing extreme conditions on sanctuary that mean that the practice is curtailed, controlled and the majority deterred. The chapter also drew on the Windrush scandal, presenting a current example to address how hospitality and labelling operate, and what happens to a group, such as the Windrush generation, when conditional hospitality intensifies and re-labelling occurs. The chapter revealed the power of labelling, particularly the continuous fracturing of the refugee label in order to suit the demands of consecutive British states, and how it intertwines to fit the government narrative of conditional hospitality. Significantly, the chapter identified how consecutive governments have attempted (successfully) to make the label of refugee a highly privileged label that the majority of claimants are unworthy of.

The case study examined in Chapter 4 was concerned with the British response to the Mediterranean crisis, examining the period 2014–18. Again, adopting the framework of humanitarian hospitality, facilitated by the practice of labelling, the chapter identified how Britain has projected hospitality not only beyond the territorial confines of the British state, but also the European Union, focusing specifically on narratives of the camps – 'upstream' in government language and policy. The British response to the Mediterranean crisis, was to locate the genuine refugee 'upstream', in the region surrounding Syria. This would be their focus for humanitarian hospitality, through establishing the Vulnerable Persons Resettlement Scheme, creating a dual role of humanitarianism but also containment. Specifically, the chapter has shown how, through the practice of labelling, as they were moving from Syria (or any of the myriad other refugee crises) and converging on the Mediterranean, refugees were being transformed into migrants and, most noticeably, (illegal) economic migrants. Through this transformation, Britain was able to negate responsibility for these individuals, as migrants invoke national, not international responsibility or obligations. The chapter has argued that there is a humanitarian hospitality, facilitated by labelling, that has enabled a state like Britain to externalise her response to the Mediterranean crisis, thus controlling and containing her responsibility to refugees, whilst upholding humanitarian credentials.

Chapter 5 focused on local, community responses to the Mediterranean crisis, drawing on thirty-four semi-structured interviews in order to create a counter-narrative to hospitality. By examining local, community responses to the Mediterranean crisis, the chapter provided a critique of the state-centred hospitality, presenting a grassroots movement attuned to responsibility, offering a counter-discourse, or a counter- ethics of unconditional hospitality towards the statist approach. Rather than perpetuating policies of containment and control, the chapter presented a politics of welcome and solidarity that emerged across Europe in what was called a 'summer of welcome', particularly in Britain, where individuals developed an emotional response to the unfolding crisis. Through an analysis of internal and external projections of hospitality, the chapter highlighted how humanitarian hospitality was wielded by community actors, in direct contradiction to the state approach, and how many identified their hospitality as resistance. But the chapter also addressed and identified tensions in local practices of hospitality, such as the community sponsorship approach to additionality. The chapter therefore explored the flexible and adaptive nature of humanitarian hospitality, as well as identifying an array of actors in the humanitarian and ethical practice. Indeed, through the interviews at least, Chapter 5 examined how individuals are resistant to state practices of hospitality – engaging in local practices of hospitality, either internally or projecting their practice externally, as a form of resistance.

The Racialised Refugee Subject

This book is fundamental in developing a theoretical framework that can be used to analyse the intersectionality of hospitality and labelling with regards to the refugee regime, a theoretical approach that has not been partnered together previously. As such, this book stands not as a culmination of research into the hospitality practices of the British refugee regime, but rather presents itself as a starting point for further exploration and research to think further on Britain's relationship with the refugee. The book has examined how hospitality and labelling have been effectively weaponised, but there is considerable scope to explore further the intersectionality of race and the significance of colonial histories within the British (and international) refugee regime. For, it is important to remember that the UNHCR, as well as being a post-Second World War, and Cold War institution, was also a colonial institution. But as Glen Peterson (2012: 327) acknowledges, the colonial origins 'seem so far to have escaped the attention of refugee scholars'. Indeed, it is prudent, when examining the refugee, not only to apply the humanitarian hospitality and the practice of labelling, but also to look for traces of colonialism that still manifest in practices towards the refugee colonial other.

In presenting this research, I am aware of the need to examine the intersectional framework of race within the British refugee regime. Race is intertwined throughout the British refugee regime, weaving itself through many of the politics towards the refugee. For the purpose of this research, however, I have purposely held back the analysis of race as a factor, instead opting to focus specifically on developing and analysing the practice of hospitality and the politics of labelling. It is only though the construction of the analytical framework developed in this book that the crucial engagement of race as a factor can be critical engaged with to a significant level. Race is an essential dimension that needs to be taken into consideration, as well as the continuing colonial legacies and power operating in the international refugee regime, where the ex-coloniser host interacts with the ex-colonised refugee. There is, therefore, scope for further research into the intersectionality of hospitality, labelling and race in regards to the British refugee regime. As Sherene Razack (2008) argues,

> We need to examine how we explain to ourselves the social hierarchies that surround us. We need to ask: where am I in this picture? Am I positioning myself as a saviour of less fortunate people? As the progressive one? As more subordinated? As innocent? These are moves of superiority and we need to reach beyond them . . . Accountability begins with tracing relations of privilege and penalty. It cannot proceed unless we examine our complicity.

Niklaus Steiner (2001) highlighted that no one in Europe is arguing to have asylum abolished. Yet British governments between 1990 and 2018, through the practice of humanitarian hospitality and facilitated by the politics of labelling, are doing all in their power to operate a policy of diminishing engagement. The refugee during the twentieth century was a demonised figure, and in the twenty-first century the term refugee has become a fractured, hierarchical label connected to geographies of exclusion that allow the British state to uphold practices of humanitarianism, whilst simultaneously grounding their aid in deterrence and containment. There is resistance to the state approach though, with individuals and communities in Britain challenging the approaches to the refugee and holding states to account. The book has highlighted the centrality of labelling within the British refugee process, and the power that labelling can have in determining the course of action when it comes to state responses to refugees – be it the Mediterranean or the Channel crossing incidents. Words matter, labels matter, as they are intertwined and bound into the practice of hospitality, as a means for states to maintain control of and resistance to the figure of the refugee. The framework of externalised humanitarian hospitality and labelling is an effective one in order to examine and explore further the British refugee regime, revealing challenges and critiques regarding identity, power, responsibility and security. Yet it is not a fixed analysis – it can be adapted further. For today's refugee is the same as yesterday's refugee, or last century's refugee – unwelcome and viewed with suspicion by the host, while the global crisis of refugees is not abating. Now more than ever we need to be examining, challenging and critiquing refugee practices to create a more humane, sustainable and compassionate system, one that does not privilege containment or hierarchies of suffering.

BIBLIOGRAPHY

Interviews

Alonso-Gabizóa, C., Volunteer for Mid-Wales Refugee Action Group, interview conducted in Machynlleth, 23 May 2018.

Anonymous 1, Volunteer for Help Refugees, interview via written answers, 28 June 2018.

Anonymous 2, Volunteer translator from Cardiff, Skype interview, 12 June 2018.

Anonymous 3, Volunteer for Cardiff and Vale Sanctuary Support, interview conducted in Cardiff, 28 July 2018.

Ashton, G., Volunteer for Mid-Wales Refugee Action Group, interview conducted in Machynlleth, 23 May 2018.

Aziz, S. Q., Coordinator for Cardiff and Vale Sanctuary Support, interview conducted in Cardiff, 28 July 2018.

Baver, A., Founder for Donate4Refugees, interview conducted in London, 21 June 2018.

Berry-Hart, T., Head of Aid and Advocacy for Calais Action, interview conducted in Cardiff, 29 June 2018.

Beven, L., CEO for Calais Caravans, telephone interview, 23 August 2018.

Bowler, M., Family Support Worker, Ethnic Minorities & Youth Support Team Work, interview conducted in Newtown, 1 June 2018.

Butterworth, D., Revd, Methodist Minister for Birmingham District, interview conducted in Birmingham, 26 July 2018.

Clegg, L., Coordinator at Meena, interview conducted in Birmingham, 27 July 2018.

Corbyn, J., MP for Islington North, interview conducted in London, 2 December 2013.

Crawther, M., Co-Executive for Waging Peace, interview conducted in London, 24 June 2018.

Donnelly, B., Volunteer for Chorleywood4Refugees, interview conducted in London, 18 June 2018.

Ereira, R., CEO of Solidarity with Refugees UK, interview conducted in London, 18 June 2018.

Evans, M., Volunteer for Riverside Refugee Kitchen and OASIS Hub, interview conducted in Cardiff, 27 June 2018.

Farooq, Y., Social Coordinator for Refugee Connection, interview conducted in London, 22 June 2018.

Fleming, C., Founder of Refugee Connection, interview conducted in London, 22 June 2018.

Gohil, C., Trustee of People not Borders, Skype interview, 4 June 2018.

Hammel, A., Trustee of Aberaid, interview conducted in Aberystwyth, 15 May 2018.

Houghton, P., Volunteer for 1FamilyCardiff, interview conducted in Cardiff, 29 June 2018.

Hutchings, P., CEO of Refugee Support Europe, Skype interview, 25 June 2018.

Jonsson, E., Project Manager of Sponsorship Refugees and Vice-Chair of Herne Hill Welcome Refugees, interview conducted in London, 19 June 2018.

Kenny, L., Treasurer of Kings Heath Action for Refugees, Birmingham, Skype interview, 4 September 2018.

Khan, A., Lawyer for Hope Projects, Birmingham, telephone interview conducted, 26 July 2018.

Lalor, D., Volunteer for Mid-Wales Refugee Action Group, interview conducted in Machynlleth, 23 May 2018.

McCormack, M., Trustee for Refugee Action Leeds and member of End Child Detention Now, Skype interview conducted on 24 January 2014.

Nelms, C., Volunteer for Riverside Refugee Kitchen, interview conducted in Cardiff, 27 June 2018.

Roach, B., Minister for State for Asylum and Immigration (July 1999 – June 2001), telephone interview conducted on 11 May 2012.

Sverdov, M., Volunteer for Mid-Wales Refugee Action Group, interview conducted in Machynlleth, 23 May 2018.

Talbot, R., Board member for Refugees at Home, Skype interview, 25 June 2018.

Vincentelli, M., Trustee of Aberaid, interview conducted in Aberystwyth, 22 November 2017.

Primary and Secondary Material

Abbas, M. S. (2019), 'Conflating the Muslim refugees and the terror suspect responses to the Syrian refugee "crisis" in Brexit Britain', *Journal of Ethnic and Racial Studies*, 42(14): 2450–69.

Abbott, D. (2000), Hansard, House of Commons Debate, Asylum Seekers, 12 April, vol. 348, cc. 426–73, <http://hansard.millbanksystems.com/commons/2000/apr/12/asylum-seekers#S6CV0348P0_20000412_HOC_302>, col. 459 (last accessed 10 April 2019).

Al Jazeera (2015a), 'Dozens of refugees found dead in truck in Austria', 27 August, <https://www.aljazeera.com/news/2015/08/dozens-refugees-dead-truck-austria-150827094349613.html> (last accessed 16 June 2018).

Al Jazeera (2015b), 'Hungary seals off southern border to refugees', 17 October, <http://www.aljazeera.com/news/2015/10/hungary-seals-southern-border-refugees-151017001552794.html> (last accessed 7 June 2016).

Amnesty International (2016), 'Refugees Welcome Index shows government refugee policies out of touch with public opinion', <https://www.amnesty.org/en/latest/news/2016/05/refugees-welcome-index-shows-government-refugee-policies-out-of-touch/> (last accessed 28 August 2018).

Amnesty International (n.d.), 'The World's refugees in numbers', <https://www.amnesty.org/en/what-we-do/refugees-asylum-seekers-and-migrants/global-refugee-crisis-statistics-and-facts/> (last accessed 3 July 2019).

Arendt, H. ([1951] 2003), *The Origins of Totalitarianism*, London: Harvest Books.

Athwal, H. (2018), 'The lethal consequences of the "hostile environment"', *Institute of Race Relations*, <http://www.irr.org.uk/news/the-lethal-consequences-of-the-hostile-environment/> (last accessed 31 January 2020).

Baker, K. (1991), Hansard, House of Commons Debate, Asylum, 2 July, vol. 194, ccl. 165–78, <http://hansard.millbanksystems.com/commons/1991/jul/02/asylum#S6CV0194P0_19910702_HOC_158> (last accessed 1 November 2014).

Barnett, M. N. and M. Finnemore (1999), 'The politics, power and pathologies of international organizations', *International Organization*, 53(4): 699–732.

Baroness Anelay of St John (2014) Hansard, House of Lords Written Answer 'Mediterranean Sea', 15 October, col. WA41, <http://www.publications.parliament.uk/pa/ld201415/ldhansrd/text/141015w0001.htm#14101579000032> (last accessed 4 November 2014).

BBC News (2013), 'Italy boat sinking: hundreds feared dead off Lampedusa', 3 October, <https://www.bbc.co.uk/news/world-europe-24380247> (last accessed 3 July 2019).

BBC News (2015a), 'Mediterranean migrant deaths: EU faces renewed pressure', 20 April, <https://www.bbc.co.uk/news/world-europe-32371348> (last accessed 3 July 2019).

BBC News (2015b), 'David Cameron criticised over migrant "swarm" language', BBC News, 30 July, <http://www.bbc.co.uk/news/uk-politics-33716501> (last accessed 3 October 2017).

BBC News (2016), 'David Cameron: UK to resettle child refugees from Europe', 4 May <http://www.bbc.co.uk/news/uk-36200366> (last accessed 3 July 2016).

BBC News (2017), 'Rohingya crisis: UN rights chief "cannot rule out genocide"', 5 December, <https://www.bbc.co.uk/news/world-asia-42234469> (last accessed 25 August 2018).

BBC News (2018), 'Five migrant boats rescued in English Channel', 25 December, <https://www.bbc.co.uk/news/uk-england-kent-46679414> (last accessed 6 July 2019).

BBC News (2019), 'Sajid Javid under fire over Channel migrant comments', 21 February, <https://www.bbc.co.uk/news/uk-politics-46738126> (last accessed 6 July 2019).

Beck, U. (2002), 'The terrorist threat: world risk society revisited', *Theory, Culture and Society*, 19(4): 39–55.

Becker, H. (1991), *Outsiders, Studies in the Sociology of Deviance*, New York: The Free Press.

Behrman, S. (2018), 'Refugee law as a means of control', *Journal of Refugee Studies*, 32(1): 42–62.

Berry-Hart, T. (2018), 'People to people: the volunteer phenomenon', *Refugee History*, 19 June, <http://refugeehistory.org/blog/2018/6/19/people-to-people-the-volunteer-phenomenon> (last accessed 17 July 2018).

Betts, A. and J. Milner (2007), 'The externalisation of EU asylum policy: the position of African states', Danish Institute for International Studies, DIIS Brief, <http://www.temaasyl.se/Documents/Forskning/Forskningsstudier/The%20externalisation%20of%20EU%20Asylum%20Policy.%20The%20position%20of%20African%20States.pdf> (last accessed 21 January 2020).

Betts, A. and P. Collier (2017), *Refugee: Transforming a Broken Refugee System*, Milton Keynes: Allen Lane.

Bhabha, H. K. (1994), *The Location of Culture*, London: Routledge.

Bialasiewicz, L. (2012), 'Off-shoring and out-sourcing the borders of EUrope: Libya and EU border work in the Mediterranean', *Geopolitics*, 17(4): 843–66.

Blair, T. (2010), *A Journey*, London: Hutchinson.

Bohmer, C. and A. Shuman (2008), *Rejecting Refugees: Political Asylum in the 21st Century*, London: Routledge.

Boltanski, L. (1999), *Distant Suffering: Morality, Media and Politics*, Cambridge: Cambridge University Press.

Borradori, G. (2003), *Philosophy in a Time of Terror: Dialogue with Jurgen Habermas and Jacques Derrida*, Chicago: University of Chicago Press.

Bowling, B. and S. Westenra (2018), 'A really hostile environment: adiaphorization, global policing and the crimmigration control system', *Theoretical Criminology*, 1 June, 1–21.

Brokenshire, J. (2015), Hansard, House of Commons Debate, European Agenda on Migration, 14 Dec 2015, vol. 603, col. 1355, <https://hansard.parliament.uk/commons/2015-12-14/debates/15121441000002/EuropeanAgendaOnMigration> (last accessed 31 January 2020).

Brun, C. (2010) 'Hospitality: becoming "IDPs" and "Host" in protracted displacements', *Journal of Refugee Studies*, 23(3): 337–55.

Bryman, A. (2008), *Social Research Methods*, 3rd edn, Oxford: Oxford University Press.

Bulley, D. (2009), *Ethics as Foreign Policy: Britain, the EU and the Other*, London: Routledge.

Bulley, D. (2017), *Migration, Ethics and Power*, London: Sage Publications.

Cameron, D. (2014), Hansard, Prime Ministers Engagements, House of Commons, HC Deb 29 January, vol. 574, col. 851. <https://hansard.parliament.uk/commons/2014-01-29/debates/14012950000002/OralAnswersToQuestions> (last accessed 10 April 2019).

Cameron, D. (2015a), Hansard, House of Commons Debate, Tunisia and the European Council, 29 June, vol. 597, col. 1180, <https://publications.parliament.uk/pa/cm201516/cmhansrd/cm150629/debtext/150629-0001.htm#1506295000001> (last accessed 31 January 2020).

Cameron, D. (2015b), Hansard, House of Commons Debate, Syria: Refugees and Counter-Terrorism, 7 September, vol. 599, col. 24. <http://www.publications.parliament.uk/pa/cm201516/cmhansrd/cm150907/debtext/150907-0001.htm#1509074000002> (last accessed 10 January 2016).

Cameron, D. (2015c), Hansard, Prime Ministers Engagements, House of Commons, HC Deb, 9 September, vol. 599, col. 397. <https://publications.parliament.uk/pa/cm201516/cmhansrd/cm150907/debindx/150907-x.htm> (last accessed 5 April 2019).

Cameron, D. (2016a), Hansard, House of Commons Debate, European Council, 21 March, vol. 607, col. 1244, <https://publications.parliament.uk/pa/cm201516/cmhansrd/cm160321/debindx/160321-x.htm> (last accessed 31 January 2020).

Cameron, D. (2016b), Hansard, House of Commons Debate, Prime Ministers Engagements, 3 June, vol. 596, col. 583, <http://hansard.parliament.uk/commons/2015-06-03/debates/15060324000006/OralAnwersToQuestions> (last accessed 2 September 2016).

Cavallar, G. (2002), *The Rights of Strangers: Theories of International Hospitality, the Global Community, and Political Justice since Vitoria*, Aldershot: Ashgate.

Citizens UK (2019), *Reaction: UK's Refugee Scheme Extended*, 17 June, <https://www.citizensuk.org/reaction_uk_s_refugee_scheme_extended> (last accessed 2 February 2020).

Clarke, K. (1992) Hansard, House of Commons Debate, Asylum and Immigration Appeals Bill, 2 November, vol. 213, ccl. 21–120. <http://hansard.millbanksystems.com/commons/1992/nov/02/asylum-and-immigration-appeals-bill#S6CV0213P0_19921102_HOC_140> (last accessed 3 November 2013).

Cole, G. (2017), 'Beyond labelling: rethinking the role and value of the refugee 'label' through semiotics', *Journal of Refugee Studies*, 31(1): 1–21.

Connolly, W. E. (1983), 'Discipline, politics and ambiguity', *Political Theory*, 11(3): 325–41.

Conservative Manifesto (2017), 'Forward together: our plan for a stronger Britain and a prosperous future', Conservative Manifesto, Conservative Party, <https://www.conservatives.com/manifesto> (last accessed 1 November 2017).

Costello, C. and M. Mouzourakis (2016), 'EU law and the detainability of asylum-seekers', *Refugee Studies Quarterly*, 35(1): 47–73.

Council of Europe (2011), 'Committee on Migration, Refugees and Population: Report on Visit to Lampedusa', <http://assembly.coe.int/CommitteeDocs/2011/amahlarg03_REV2_2011.pdf> (last accessed 19 March 2018).

Crawley, H. (2010), Chance or Choice? Understanding why asylum-seekers come to the UK, Refugee Council, <http://www.refugeecouncil.org.uk/assets/0001/5702/rcchance.pdf> (last accessed 2 August 2015).

Crawley, H., F. Duvell, K. Jones, S. McMahon, and N. Sigano (2016), *Destination Europe? Understanding the Dynamics and Drivers of Mediterranean Migration in 2015*, MEDMIG Final Report, <http://www.medmig.info/wp-content/uploads/2016/12/research-brief-destination-europe.pdf> (last accessed 16 December 2017).

Daddow, O. (2013), 'Margaret Thatcher, Tony Blair and the Eurosceptic tradition in Britain', *British Journal of Politics and International Relations*, 15(2): 210–27.

Darling, A. (1991), Hansard, House of Commons Debate, Asylum Bill, 13 November, vol. 198, ccl. 82–181, <http://hansard.millbanksystems.com/commons/1991/nov/13/asylum-bill#S6CV0198P0_19911113_HOC_214> (last accessed 1 November 2013).

Darling, J. (2009), 'Becoming bare life: asylum, hospitality and the politics of the encampment', *Environment and Planning D: Society and Space*, 27(4): 649–65.

Derrida, J. (1993), *Aporias: Dying – Awaiting at the "Limits of Truth"*, Stanford, CA: Stanford University Press.

Derrida, J. (1995), *The Gift of Death*, London: University of Chicago Press.

Derrida, J. (1997), 'Politics and friendship: a discussion with Jacques Derrida', <http://www.dariaroithmayr.com/pdfs/assignments/Politics%20and%20Friendship.pdf> (last accessed 10 May 2019).

Derrida, J. (1999a), *Adieu to Immanuel Levinas*, Stanford, CA: Stanford University Press.

Derrida, D. (1999b), 'Hospitality, justice and responsibility: a dialogue with Jacques Derrida', in R. Kearney and M. Dooley, *Questioning Ethics: Contemporary Debates in Philosophy*, London, Routledge, pp. 65–83.

Derrida, J. (2000), *Of Hospitality: Anne Dufourmantelle invites Jacques Derrida to Respond*, Stanford, CA: Stanford University Press.

Derrida, J. (2001), *On Cosmopolitanism and Forgiveness*, London: Routledge.

Derrida, J. (2003), 'Autoimmunity: real and symbolic suicides: a dialogue with Jacques Derrida', in G. Borradori, *Philosophy in a Time of Terror: Dialogues with Jurgen Habermas and Jacques Derrida*, Chicago: University of Chicago Press, pp. 85–136.

Derrida, J. (2005a), 'The principle of hospitality', *Parallax*, 11(1): 6–9.

Derrida, J. (2005b), *Paper Machine*, Stanford, CA: Stanford University Press.

Doty, R. (2006) 'Fronteras compasivas and the ethics of unconditional hospitality', *Millennium*, 35(1): 53–74.

Duncan-Smith, I. (1992), Hansard, House of Commons Debates, Asylum and Immigration Bill, 2 November, vol. 213, ccl. 21–120. <http://hansard.millbanksystems.com/commons/1992/nov/02/asylum-and-immigration-appeals-bill#S6CV0213P0_19921102_HOC_140> (last accessed 3 November 2013).

Eaton, T. (2017), *Europe's Flawed Thinking on Mediterranean Migration*, Chatham House, <https://www.chathamhouse.org/expert/

comment/europe-s-flawed-thinking-mediterranean-migration>
(last accessed 18 September 2017).

Electronic Immigration Network, (2018), 'Immigration minister: Government is keeping "compliant environment" policies despite Windrush', 5 September, <https://www.ein.org.uk/news/immigration-minister-government-keeping-compliant-environment-policies-despite-windrush> (last accessed 7 August 2019).

Elgot, J. and P. Walker (2019), 'Javid under fire over "illegal" cross-Channel asylum seekers claim', *The Guardian*, 2 January, <https://www.theguardian.com/politics/2019/jan/02/people-crossing-channel-not-genuine-asylum-seekers-javid> (last accessed 21 February 2019).

Ellwood, T. (2015), Hansard, House of Commons Debate, Lebanon (Syrian Refugees), 20 January, vol. 591, col. 74, <http://hansard.parliament.uk/commons/2015-01-20/debates/1501204000005/OralAnswersToQuestions> (last accessed 10 June 2016).

Ereira, R. (2015), 'Why I had to organise a march showing Briton's solidarity with refugees', *The Guardian*, 4 September, <https://www.theguardian.com/commentisfree/2015/sep/04/organise-london-march-britons-solidarity-refugees-london-facebook> (last accessed 17 June 2017).

European Union (2003), Dublin II Regulation, C343/2003, <http://eur-lex.europa.eu/legal-content/EN/TXT/HTML/?uri=URISERV:l33153&from=EN> (last accessed 4 March 2016).

Fekete, L. (2001), 'The emergence of Xeno-racism', *Race and Class*, 42(2): 23–40.

Fekete, L. (2018), 'Migrants, borders and the criminalisation of solidarity in the EU', *Race and Class*, 59(4): 65–83.

Foucault, M. ([1975] 1991), *Discipline and Punish: The Birth of the Prison*, London: Penguin Books.

Foucault, M. (1994), *Power: Essential Works of Foucault 1954–1984*, London, Penguin Books.

Foucault, M. (2009), 'Alternatives to the prison: dissemination or decline of societal control', *Theory, Culture, Society*, 26(12): 12–24.

Friedman, E. and R. Klein (2008), *Reluctant Refugee: The Story of Asylum in Britain*, London: British Library Publications.

Friese, H. (2010), 'The limits of hospitality: political philosophy, undocumented migration and the local arena', *European Journal of Social Theory*, 13(3): 323–41.

Gartkisch, M., J. Heidingsfelder and M. Beckman (2017),'Third sector organisations and migration: a systematic literature review on the contribution of third sector organisations in view of flight, migration and refugee crises', *Voluntas*, (28)(5): 1839–80.

Gibney, M. (2004), *The Ethics and Politics of Asylum: Liberal Democracy and the Response to Refugees*, Cambridge: Cambridge University Press.

Gibney, M. (2008), 'Asylum and the expansion of deportation in the United Kingdom', *Government and Opposition*, 43(2): 146–67.

Gibney, M. (2014), 'Asylum: principled hypocrisy', in B. Anderson and M. Keith (eds) *Migration: A COMPAS Anthology*, Oxford: COMPAS, pp. 163–4.

Gill, N. (2016), *Nothing Personal? Geographies of Governing and Activism in the British Asylum System*, Oxford: John Wiley.

Gill, N. (2018), 'The suppression of welcome', *Fennia*, 196(1): 88–9.

Global Refugee Sponsorship Initiative (2017), *Building Blocks of Community Sponsorship: Guidebook and Planning Tools Based on Canada's Model*, 18 September, <http://www.refugeesponsorship.org/ajax/?comaction=guidebook-print&enumLang=en&chapter=0&area=0&section=0&consideration=0> (last accessed 7 September 2018).

Goodhall, C. (2010), 'The coming of the stranger: asylum seekers, trust and hospitality in a British city', *UN High Commissioner for Refugees*, Research Paper no. 195, November, <http://www.refworld.org/pdfid/4d0210a92.pdf> (last accessed 22 April 2014).

Goodwin-Gill, G. (1999), 'Refugee identity and protection's fading prospect', in F. Nicholson and P. Twomey, *Refugee Rights and Realities: Evolving International Concepts and Regimes*, Cambridge: Cambridge University Press.

Gower, M. (2015), Parliamentary Briefing Paper: Asylum support: accommodation and financial support for asylum seeker, Number 1909, October, <http://researchbriefings.parliament.uk/ResearchBriefing/Summary/SN06805> (last accessed 4 March 2016).

Grahl-Madesn, A. (1983), 'Identifying the world's refugees', *ANNALS of the American Academy of Political and Social Science*, 467(1): 11–23.

Grant, P. (2015), Hansard, House of Commons Debate, European Agenda on Migration, 14 December, vol. 603, col. 1365, <http://hansard.parliament.uk/commons/2015-12-14/debates/15121441000002/EuropeanAgendaOnMigration> (last accessed 10 June 2016).

Greening, J. (2015), Hansard, House of Commons Debate, Illegal Migration, 3 June, vol. 596, col. 574, <https://publications.parliament.uk/pa/cm201516/cmhansrd/cm150603/debtext/150603-0001.htm#15060324000721> (last accessed 31 January 2020).

Greening, J. (2016), Hansard, House of Commons Debate, Syria: UK's Response, 8 February, vol. 604, col. 1323, <http://hansard.parliament.uk/commons/2016-02-08/debates/1602085000002/SyrianCrisisUKResponse> (last accessed 7 September 2016).

Gupte, J. and L. Mehta (2007), 'Disjuncture in labelling refugees and oustees', in J. Moncrieffe and R. Eyben, *The Power of Labelling: How People Are Categorised and Why it Matters*, London: Earthscan, pp. 64–79.

Hall, S. (1978), *Policing the Crisis: Mugging, the State and Law and Order*, London: Macmillan Press.

Hammond, P. (2015), Hansard, House of Commons Debate, Britain in the World, 1 June, vol. 596, col. 320, <http://hansard.parliament.uk/commons/2015-06-01/debates/1506013000003/BritainInTheWorld> (last accessed 4 June 2016).

Harper, M. (2013), Home Office, Written Statement to Parliament, 6 June. <https://www.gov.uk/government/speeches/rates-of-asylum-support> (last accessed 6 June 2015).

Harvey, C. J. (2000), 'Dissident voices: refugees, human rights and asylum in Europe', *Social and Legal Studies*, 9(3): 367–96.

Hathaway, J. C. (1991), *The Law of Refugee Studies*, Toronto, ON, Canada: Butterworths.

Hatton, T. J. (2008), 'The rise and fall of asylum: what happened and why?', *Centre for Economic Policy Research*, Discussion Paper Series no. 6752, London: Centre for Economic Policy Research.

Hawkins, O. (2014), Parliamentary briefing: Asylum statistics (Updated), SN/SG/1403, June, <www.parliament.uk/briefing-papers/SN01403.pdf> (last accessed 10 January 2015).

Hehir, A. (2010), *Humanitarian Intervention: An Introduction*, Palgrave Macmillan: Basingstoke.

Helton, A. C. (2003), *The Price of Indifference: Refugee and Humanitarian Action in the New Century*, Oxford: Oxford University Press.

Hollobone, P. (2010). Hansard, House of Commons Debate, Asylum Applications, 28 June, col. 554, <http://www.publications. parliament.uk/pa/cm201011/cmhansrd/cm100628/ debtext/100628-0002.htm#1006288000021> (last accessed 10 December 2014).

Holloway, A. (2015), Hansard, House of Commons Debate, Asylum (Unaccompanied Children Displaced by Conflict), 8 December, vol. 599, col. 268, <http://hansards.parliament.uk/ common/2015-12-08/debates/1512084300000/Asylum(Unacc ompaniedChildrenDisplacedByConflict)> (last accessed 8 June 2016).

Home Office (2017), *Community Sponsorship Guidance for Prospective Sponsors*, July, <https://assets.publishing.service.gov.uk/govern- ment/uploads/system/uploads/attachment_data/file/626810/ Community_sponsorship_guidance_for_prospective_sponsors_ July_2017.pdf>(last accessed 25 August 2018).

Home Office (2018), 'Home Secretary bolsters Border Force fleet in the Channel', 31 December, <https://www.gov.uk/government/ news/home-secretary-bolsters-border-force-fleet-in-the- channel> (last accessed 6 July 2019).

Home Office (2019), 'Funding instructions for local authorities in the support of the United Kingdoms Resettlement Schemes, Financial Year, 2019–2020', <https://www.gov.uk/government/ publications/uk-resettlement-programmes-funding-instruction- 2019-to-2020> (last accessed 5 July 2019).

Home Office (2019), 'STATEMENT by Sajid Javid: Migrant crossing', 7 January <https://www.gov.uk/government/speeches/statement- migrant-crossings> (last accessed 21 June 2019).

Horsch, E. (1985), 'Labelling and the language of international development', *Development and Change*, 16(3): 503–14.

House of Commons (2017), House of Lords Joint Committee on Human Rights, 'Windrush Generation Detention', 6th Report, <https://publications.parliament.uk/pa/jt201719/jtselect/jtrights/1034/103403.htm#_idTextAnchor000> (last accessed 20 February 2019).

House of Commons (2018), Home Affairs Committee, 'Asylum accommodation: replacing COMPASS', <https://publications.parliament.uk/pa/cm201719/cmselect/cmhaff/1758/1758.pdf> (last accessed 10 December 2018).

House of Commons International Development Committee (2016), 'Syrian refugee crisis: first report of session 2015–2016', HC 463, 2016, <https://publications.parliament.uk/pa/cm201516/cmselect/cmintdev/902/902.pdf> (last accessed 20 June 2017).

House of Commons Parliament TV (2015), Prime Minister's Question Time, Parliament Live TV, 3 June, <http://parliamentlive.tv/event/index/00871386-3032-4bda-bfe5-7af41437696e?in=12:01:13> (last accessed 10 June 2015).

Howard, M. (1995a), Hansard, House of Commons Debate, Asylum and Immigration, 20 November, <http://www.publications.parliament.uk/pa/cm199596/cmhansrd/vo951120/debtext/51120-05.htm> (last accessed 11 November 2013).

Howard, M. (1995b), Hansard, House of Commons Debate, Asylum and Immigration Bill, 11 December, vol. 268, ccl. 699–808, <http://hansard.millbanksystems.com/commons/1995/dec/11/asylum-and-immigration-bill#S6CV0268P0_19951211_HOC_389> (last accessed 2 June 2019).

Hughes, B. (2004), Hansard, House of Commons Written Answer, Asylum Policy, 23 February, col. 225w, <http://www.publications.parliament.uk/pa/cm200304/cmhansrd/vo040223/text/40223w56.htm> (last accessed 4 March 2016).

Hyndman, J. (2003), 'Preventive, palliative or punitive? Safe spaces in Bosnia-Herzegovina, Somalia, and Sri Lanka', *Journal of Refugee Studies*, 16(2): 167–85.

Ibrahim, Y. and A. Howarth (2018a), 'Communicating the "migrant" other as risk: space, EU and expanding borders', *Journal of Risk Research*, 21(12): 1465–86.

Ibrhamin, Y. and A. Howarth (2018b), 'Review of humanitarian refuge in the United Kingdom: sanctuary', Asylum and the refugee crisis, *Politics and Policy*, 46(3): 348–91.

Institute for Race Relations (2017), 'Humanitarianism: the unacceptable face of solidarity', <http://s3-eu-west-2.amazonaws.com/wpmedia.outlandish.com/irr/2017/11/10092853/Humanitarianism_the_unacceptable_face_of_solidarity.pdf> (last accessed 20 February 2019).

Institute for Race Relations (2018), 'Fighting the hostile environment: interview with Bethan Lant of Praxis', <http://www.irr.org.uk/news/fighting-the-hostile-environment-interview-with-bethan-lant-of-praxis/> (last accessed 20 February 2019).

International Development Committee (2015), House of Commons, Syrian Refugee Crisis, First Report of Session 2015–2016, HC463, <https://publications.parliament.uk/pa/cm201516/cmselect/cmintdev/463/463.pdf> (last accessed 24 June 2017).

Jabri, V. (2013), *The Postcolonial Subject: Claiming Politics/Governing Others in Late Modernity*, London: Routledge.

Jenkins, B. (2015), Hansard, House of Commons Debate, Defence, 8 June, vol. 595, col. 906, <https://hansard.parliament.uk/commons/2015-06-08/debates/1506082000004/OralAnswerToQuestion> (last accessed 6 June 2016).

Joint Select Committee on Human Rights (2018), The Joint Committee on Human Rights publishes Windrush generation detention report, 29 June, <https://www.parliament.uk/business/committees/committees-a-z/joint-select/human-rights-committee/news-parliament-2017/windrush-report-publication17-19/> (last accessed 31 January 2020).

Jones, R. (2016), *Violent Borders: Refugees and the Right to Move*, London: Verso.

Kakoliris, G. (2015), 'Jacques Derrida on the ethics of hospitality', in E. Imafidon (ed.), *The Ethics of Subjectivity*, London: Palgrave Macmillan, pp. 144–56.

Kant, K. (1795), 'Perpetual peace: a philosophical sketch', <https://slought.org/media/files/perpetual_peace.pdf> (last accessed 12 July 2019).

Karakayali, S. and J. O. Kleist (2016), 'Volunteer and Asylum Seekers', *Forced Migration Review*, 51: 65–7.

Kennedy, D. (2004), *The Dark Sides of Virtue*, Oxford: Princeton University Press.

Kirkwood, S. (2017), 'The humanisation of refugees: a discourse analysis of UK parliamentary debates on the European refugee crisis', *Journal of Community and Applied Social Psychology*, 27(2): 115–25.

Linklater, A. (2007), 'Distant suffering and cosmopolitan obligations', *International Politics*, 44(1): 19–36.

Little, A. and N. Vaughan-Williams (2016), 'Stopping the boats, saving lives, securing subjects: humanitarian borders in Europe and Australia', *European Journal of International Relations*, 23(3): 533–56.

Lord Jakobovits, Hansard, House of Lords Debates, Asylum and Immigration Appeals Bill. 11 March 1993, vol. 543, ccl. 145-95, http://hansard.millbanksystems.com/lords/1993/mar/11/asylum-and-immigration-appeals-bill#S5LV0543P0_19930311_HOL_82 (last accessed 31 January 2020).

Ludwig, B. (2013), '"Wiping the refugee dust from my feet": advantages and burdens of refugee status and the refugee label', *International Migration*, 54(1): 1–18.

Lynch, P., J. G. Molz, A. Macintost, P. Lugosi and C. Lashley (2011), 'Theorizing hospitality', *Hospitality and Society*, 1(1): 3–24.

McFadyen, G. (2016), 'The language of labelling and the politics of hostipitality in the British asylum system', *British Journal of Politics and International Relations*, 18(3): 599–617.

McFadyen, G. (2019), 'Memory, language and silence: barriers to refuge within the British asylum system', *Journal of Immigrant and Refugee Studies*, 17(2): 168–84.

McGee, D. and Pelham, J. (2018), 'Politics at play: locating human rights, refugees and grassroots humanitarianism in the Calais Jungle', *Leisure Studies*, 37(1): 22-35.

McGuiness, T. (2017), *The UK Response to the Syrian refugee crisis*, House of Commons Briefing Paper, Number 06805, 14 June, <https://researchbriefings.parliament.uk/ResearchBriefing/Summary/SN06805>, (last accessed 27 June 2017).

McKinnon, S. (2008), 'Unsettling resettlement: problematizing "lost boys of Sudan" resettlement and identity', *Western Journal of Communication*, 72(4): 397–414.

Macleod, E. (2016) 'The Syrian refugee situation: sign of new world disorder?', Gramnet Speak Series, University of Glasgow, 17 May.

Malins, H. (2003), Hansard, House of Commons Debate, Asylum and Immigration, (Treatment of Claimants, etc.) Bill, 17 December, vol. 415, cc1. 587–620, <http://hansard.millbanksystems.com/commons/2003/dec/17/asylum-and-immigration-treatment-of#S6CV0415P1_20031217_HOC_145> (last accessed 7 July 2018).

Malkki, L. (2015), *The Need to Help: The Domestic Art of International Humanitarianism*, London: Duke University Press.

Maniatis, G. (2017), 'A message from Wales on refugees: "people are very keen to help"', *Open Society Foundation*, 14 July, <https://www.opensocietyfoundations.org/voices/message-wales-refugees-people-are-very-keen-help> (last accessed 7 September 2018).

Maniatis, G. and J. Bond (2018), 'A new model for refugee resettlement puts people first, and gathers support', *Open Society Foundation*, 17 July, <https://www.opensocietyfoundations.org/voices/new-model-refugee-resettlement-puts-people-first-and-gathers-support> (last accessed 7 September 2018).

Marfleet, P. (2006), *Refugees in a Global Era*, Basingstoke: Palgrave.

Marino, S. (2016), 'What are we going to do about them? The centrality of border in Fortress Europe', *Networking Knowledge Journal*, 9(4): 1–12.

May, T. (2014), Hansard, House of Commons Debate, UN Syrian Refugee Programme, 29 January, vol. 574, col. 889, <https://hansard.parliament.uk/commons/2014-01-29/debates/14012952000001/UNHCRSyrianRefugeesProgramme> (last accessed 2 June 2016).

May, T. (2015a), House of Commons Debate, Border Management (Calais), 24 June 2015, vol. 597, col. 902, <https://publications.parliament.uk/pa/cm201516/cmhansrd/cm150624/debtext/150624-0001.htm#15062462001758> (last accessed 31 January 2020).

May, T. (2015b), Speech to the Conservative Party Conference, 6 October, <http://www.independent.co.uk/news/uk/politics/

theresa-may-s-speech-to-the-conservative-party-conference-in-full-a6681901.html> (last accessed 8 June 2016).

Mayblin, L. (2017), *Asylum After Empire: Colonial Legacies in Politics of Asylum Seeking*, London: Rowman and Littlefield.

Mayblin, L. and P. James (2018), 'Asylum and refugee support in the UK: civil society filling the gaps?', *Journal of Ethnic and Migration Studies*, 45(3): 375–94.

Mayer, M. (2018), 'Cities as sites of refuge and resistance', *European Urban and Regional Studies*, 25(3): 232–49.

Mediterranean Migration Research Project (2016), *Understanding the Dynamics of Migration to Greece and the EU*, Research Brief 02, <http://www.medmig.info/research-brief-02-understanding-the-dynamics-of-migration-to-greece-and-the-eu/> (last accessed 25 August 2018).

Merolla, J., S. K. Ramakrishnan and C. Haynes (2013), '"Illegal," "undocumented," or "unauthorized": equivalency and frames, issue frames and public opinion on immigration', *Perspectives on Politics*, 11(3): 789–807.

Michalski, W. (2015), 'Mediterranean crisis: the big haggle', *Human Rights Watch*, 24 June, <https://www.hrw.org/news/2015/06/24/mediterranean-crisis-big-haggle> (last accessed 20 October 2017).

Moncrieffe, J. (2006), 'The power of stigma: encounters with "street children" and "Restavecs" in Haiti', *Institute of Development Studies (IDS) Bulletin*, 37(6): 34–46.

Moncrieffe, J. (2007), 'Introduction', in J. Moncrieffe and R. Eyben, *The Power of Labelling: How People Are Categorised and Why it Matters*, London: Earthscan, pp. 1–17.

Mountz, A. (2011), 'The enforcement archipelago: detention, haunting, and asylum on islands', *Political Geography*, 30(3): 118–28.

Mountz, A. and L. Briskman (2012), 'Introducing island detentions: the placement of asylum seekers and migrants on islands', *Shima: The International Journal of Research into Island Cultures*, 6(2): 21–6.

Mulvey, G. (2010), 'When policy creates policies: the problematizing of immigration and the consequences for refugee integration', *Journal of Refugee Studies*, 23(4): 437–62.

Naylor, T. (2011), 'Deconstructing development: the use of power and pity in the international development discourse', *International Studies Quarterly*, 55(1): 177–97.

Nicholson, F. and P. Twomey (1998), *Current Issues of UK Asylum Law and Policy*, Aldershot: Ashgate.

Parker, S. (2018), '"Just eating and sleeping": asylum seekers' constructions of belonging within a restrictive policy environment', *Critical Discourse Studies*, 1–17.

Pemberton, S. (2004), 'A theory of moral indifference: understanding the production of harm by capitalist society', in P. Hillyard, C. Pantazis, S. Tombs and D. Gordon, *Beyond Criminology. Taking Harm Seriously*, London: Pluto Press, pp. 67–83.

Peterson, G. (2012), 'The uneven development of the international refugee regime in postwar Asia: evidence from China, Hong Kong and Indonesia', *Journal of Refugee Studies*, 25(3): 326–43.

Philimore, J. A. McCabe, A. S. Soteri-Proctor and R. Taylor (2010), 'Understanding the distinctiveness of small scale, third sector activity: the role of local knowledge and networks in shaping below the radar actions', Briefing Paper 33, *Third Sector Research Centre*, <http://epapers.bham.ac.uk/792/1/WP33_Understanding_the_distinctiveness_of_small_scale_TS_activity_-_Phillimore%2C_McCabe_May_10.pdf> (last accessed 10 September 2018).

Phillips, M. and T. Phillips (1998), *Windrush: The Irresistible Rise of Multi-Racial Britain*, London: Harper Collins.

Phipps, A. (2019), 'Bearing witness: the burden of individual responsibility and the rule of law', in K. Kehare, E. Alisic and J. C. Heilinger, *Responsibility for Refugees and Migration Integration*, Berlin: Deutsche National Bibliothek, pp. 9–25.

Razack, S. (2008), *Looking White People in the Eye: Gender, Race, and Culture in Courtrooms and Classrooms*, London: University of Toronto.

Rees-Mogg, J. (2015), Hansard, House of Commons Debate, European Agenda on Migration, 14 December, vol. 603, col. 1347, <https://publications.parliament.uk/pa/cm201516/cmhansrd/cm151214/debtext/151214-0003.htm#15121441000002> (last accessed 31 January 2020).

Refugee Council (2005), 'Asylum and Immigration Act 2004: an update briefing, March, <http://www.refugeecouncil.org.uk/

assets/0001/5662/ai_act_update_05> (last accessed 22 April 2014).

Refugee Council (2018), 'Refugee Council response to Channel crossing news', <https://www.refugeecouncil.org.uk/latest/news/5457_refugee_council_response_to_channel_crossing_news/> (last accessed 7 July 2019).

Refugee Council (2019), 'Latest immigration statistics published', <https://www.refugeecouncil.org.uk/latest/news/latest-immigration-statistics-published/> (last accessed 25 May 2019).

Retzlaff, S. (2005), 'What's in a name? The politics of labelling and native identity constructions', *Canadian Journal of Native Studies*, 15(2): 609–26.

Reynolds, S. (2018), 'Open arms or a clenched fist: what kind of welcome will Brexit Britain offer to refugees?', *The Progressive Policy Think Tank (IPPR) Progressive Review*, 25(1): 70–5.

Rosello, M. (2001), *Postcolonial Hospitality: The Immigrant as Guest*, California: Stanford University Press.

Said, E. [1978] (2003), *Orientalism*, London: Penguin Books.

Sales, R. (2003), '"The deserving and the undeserving?" Refugees, asylum seekers and welfare in Britain', *Critical Social Policy*, 22(3): 456–78.

Sandri, E. (2017), 'Volunteer humanitarianism: volunteers and humanitarian aid in the Jungle refugee camp Calais', *Journal of Ethnic and Migration Studies*, 44(1): 65–80.

Schofield, K. (2019), 'WATCH: Sajid Javid suggests cross-Channel asylum seekers may not be "genuine"', Politics Home, 2 January, <https://www.politicshome.com/news/uk/home-affairs/immigration/news/100823/watch-sajid-javid-suggests-cross-channel-asylum-seekers> (last accessed 5 July 2019).

Secretary of State for the Home Department (2002), *Secure Borders Safe Haven: Integration with Diversity in Modern Britain*, London: The Stationary Office, February (CM5387).

Silvereira, C. (2016), 'The representation of (illegal) migrants in the British news', *Networking Knowledge*, (9)(4): 1–16.

Simsa, R., P. Rameder, A. Aghamanoukjan and M. Totter (2018), 'Spontaneous volunteering in social crises: self-organization and coordination', *Non-profit and Voluntary Sector Quarterly*, 48(2S): 103–122.

Sjjad, T. (2018), 'What's in a name? "Refugees", "migrants" and the politics of labelling', *Race and Class*, 60(2): 40–62.

Skillington, T. (2016), 'The borders of contemporary Europe: territory, justice and rights', in A. Czajka and B. Isyar, *Europe After Derrida, Crisis and Potentiality*, Edinburgh: Edinburgh University Press, pp. 95–107.

Smith, D. (1995), *Criminology for Social Work*, Basingstoke: Macmillan.

Sponsor Refugees (2019), *Resettlement Scheme Extended! Community Sponsorship to be Additional*, 17 June, <https://www.sponsor-refugees.org/community_sponsorship_to_be_additional_as_government_announces_extension_to_resettlement_scheme> (last accessed 2 February 2020).

Squire, V. (2017), *Crossing the Mediterranean Sea by Boat: Mapping and Documenting Migratory Journeys and Experiences. Final Project Report*, Warwick: University of Warwick.

Steiner, N. (2001), 'Arguing about asylum: the complexity of refugee debates in Europe', New Issues in Refugee Research, Working Paper no. 48, <https://www.refworld.org/pdfid/4ff565292.pdf> (last accessed 13 July 2019).

Stevens, D. (1998a), 'The Asylum and Immigration Act 1996: erosion of the right to seek asylum', *Modern Law Review*, 61(2): 207–22.

Stevens, D. (1998b), 'The age of UK asylum law and policy: lessons from history?', in F. Nicholson and P. Twomey, *Current Issues of UK Asylum Law and Policy*, Aldershot: Ashgate, pp. 9–33.

Still, J. (2013), *Derrida and Hospitality: Theory and Practice*, Edinburgh: Edinburgh University Press.

Straw, J. (1999), 'Straw unveils plans to stem refugee applications', *The Guardian*, 9 February, <http://www.guardian.co.uk/uk/1999/feb/09/1> (last accessed 31 October 2010).

Straw, J. (2001), 'An effective protection regime for the twenty-first century, Speech to the Institute for Public Policy Research', *The Guardian*, 6 February. <https://www.theguardian.com/uk/2001/feb/06/immigration.immigrationandpublicservices3> (last accessed 12 July 2019).

The Committee of Public Accounts (2017), 'The Syrian Vulnerable Persons Resettlement programme', 4 January, <https://publications.

parliament.uk/pa/cm201617/cmselect/cmpubacc/768/76806.
htm> (last accessed 30 August 2017).

The Guardian (2016), 'How David Cameron's language on refugees has provoked anger', 27 January, <http://www.theguardian.com/uk-news/2016/jan/27/david-camerons-bunch-of-migrants-quip-is-latest-of-several-such-comments> (last accessed 6 June 2016).

The Independent (2015), 'Theresa May's speech to the Conservative Party Conference – in full', 6 October, <https://www.independent.co.uk/news/uk/politics/theresa-may-s-speech-to-the-conservative-party-conference-in-full-a6681901.html> (last accessed 25 August 2018).

The Mediterranean Migrant Crisis (2015), 'In Focus: The Mediterranean Migrant Crisis', House of Lords, LIF 2015/0003, <https://researchbriefings.parliament.uk/ResearchBriefing/Summary/LIF-2015-0003> (last accessed 20 July 2017).

Townshead, M. (2019), 'Cold, alone and scared: teenage refugee tells of Channel crossing', The Observer, 9 June, <https://www.theguardian.com/uk-news/2019/jun/09/teenage-refugee-tells-of-channel-crossing> (last accessed 6 July 2019).

Transnational Immigration Panel (2018), 'PPI on human rights of migrant and refugee peoples', International Public Opinion Tribunal, 22 December, <https://www.statewatch.org/news/2019/jun/PPT-London-Deliberation_FINAL.pdf> (last accessed 2 February 2019).

Turton, D. (2003), 'Conceptualising forced migration', Refugee Studies Centre Working Paper, no. 12, <http://www.rsc.ox.ac.uk/files/publications/working-paper-series/wp12-conceptualising-forced-migration-2003.pdf> (last accessed 12 June 2018).

Tyler, I. (2018), 'Deportation nation: Theresa May's hostile environment', Journal for the Study of British Cultures, 25(1).

UK Border Agency (2011), 'Considering asylum claims and assessing credibility', <http://www.ukba.homeoffice.gov.uk/sitecontent/documents/policyandlaw/asylumprocessguidance/consideringanddecidingtheclaim/guidance/considering-protection-.pdf?view=Binary> (last accessed 27 November 2013; weblink no longer available).

UN News (2017), 'UN human rights chief points to "textbook example of ethnic cleansing" in Myanmar', <https://news.un.org/en/

story/2017/09/564622-un-human-rights-chief-points-textbook-example-ethnic-cleansing-myanmar> (last accessed 2 February 2020).

United Nations High Commissioner for Refugees (UNHCR) [1951] (2006), *Convention and Protocol Relating to the Status of Refugees*, UNHCR: Geneva.

United Nations High Commissioner for Refugees (UNHCR) (2016a), Syria Regional Refugee Response, <http://data.unhcr.org/syrianrefugees/regional.php> (last accessed 7 June 2016).

United Nations High Commissioner for Refugees (UNHCR) (2016b), 'Refugees from Syria: Lebanon', http://data2.unhcr.org/en/documents/downloads/45764 (last accessed 2 February 2019).

United Nations High Commissioner for Refugees (UNHCR, 2016c), 'UNHCR Viewpoint: "Refugee" or "Migrant" – Which Is Right?', <https://unhcr.org/news/latest/2016/7/55dfoe556/unhcr-viewpoint-refugee-migrant-right.html> (last accessed 6 May 2020).

United Nations High Commissioner for Refugees (UNHCR) (2018), 'Humanitarian Principles, Emergency Handbook', <https://emergency.unhcr.org/entry/95307/humanitarian-principles> (last accessed 14 May 2018).

Van Houten, H. (2010), 'Human blacklisting: the global apartheid of the EU's external border regime', *Environment and Planning D: Society and Space*, 28(6): 957–76.

Vaughan-Williams, N. (2015), *Europe's Border Crisis: Biopolitical Security and Beyond*, Oxford: Oxford University Press.

Vigil, Y. N. and C. B. Abidi (2018), '"We" the refugees: reflections on refugee labels and identitites', *Refuge: Canada's Journal on Refugees*, 34(2): 52–60.

Wambu, O. (1998), 'Introduction', in O. Wambu (ed.), *Empire Windrush: Fifty Years of Writing About Black Britain*, London: Phoenix, pp. 19–32.

Waterson, N. (1999), Hansard, House of Commons Debates, Immigration and Asylum Bill, 16 February, vol. 326, ccl. 37–129, <http://hansard.millbanksystems.com/commons/1999/feb/22/immigration-and-asylum-bill#S6CV0326P0_19990222_HOC_181> (last accessed 13 November 2013).

Watson, M. (1991), Hansard, House of Commons Debate, Asylum Bill, 13 November, vol. 198, cc. 1082–181. <http://hansard.millbanksystems.com/commons/1991/nov/13/asylumbill#S6CV0198P0_19911113_HOC_214 > (last accessed 10 May 2014).

Webber, F. (2018a), 'On the creation of the UK's "hostile environment"', Race and Class, 60(4): 76–87.

Webber, F. (2018b), 'The Windrush generation retreat and the hostile environment', Institute of Race Relations, <http://www.irr.org.uk/news/the-windrush-generation-retreat-and-the-hostile-environment/> (last accessed 20 February 2019).

Webber, F. (2018c), 'The embedding of state hostility: a background paper on the Windrush scandal', Institute of Race Relations, Briefing Paper no. 11, <http://www.irr.org.uk/publications/issues/the-embedding-of-state-hostility-a-background-paper-on-the-windrush-scandal/> (last accessed 12 July 2019).

Wells, B. (1992), Hansard, House of Commons Debate, Asylum and Immigration Appeals Bill, 2 November, vol. 213, ccl. 21–120, <http://hansard.millbanksystems.com/commons/1992/nov/02/asylum-and-immigration-appeals-bill#S6CV0213P0_19921102_HOC_140> (last accessed 12 July 2019).

Welsh Refugee Council (2018), 'Response to the Independent Chief Inspector of Borders and Immigration call for evidence into asylum accommodation', <https://wrc.wales/sites/default/files/news/files/ICI%20Borders%20%26%20Immigration%20Call%20for%20Evidence%2C%20Asylum%20Accommodation%20Final.pdf> (last accessed 12 July 2019).

Westmoreland, M. W. (2008), 'Interruptions: Derrida and hospitality', Kritike, 2(1): 1–10.

Wilson, E. (2010), 'Protecting the unprotected: reconceptualising refugee protection through the notion of hospitality', Local-Global Journal, 8(1):100–22.

Wolfson, M. (1995), Hansard, House of Commons Debates, Asylum and Immigration Bill, 11 December, vol. 268, ccl. 699–808, <http://hansard.millbanksystems.com/commons/1995/dec/11/asylum-and-immigration-bill#S6CV0268P0_19951211_HOC_389> (last accessed 2 July 2015).

Wood, G. (1985), 'The politics of development policy labelling', Development and Change, (16)(3): 347–73.

Zetter, R. (1985), 'Refugees – access and labelling', *Development and Change*, 16(3): 429–50.

Zetter, R. (1988), 'Refugees and refugee studies – a label and an agenda', *Journal of Refugee Studies*, 1(1): 1–6.

Zetter, R. (1991), 'Labelling refugees: forming and transforming a bureaucratic identity', *Journal of Refugee Studies*, 4(1): 39–62.

Zetter, R. (2000), 'Refugees and refugee studies – a valedictory editorial', *Journal of Refugee Studies*, 13(4): 349–55.

Zetter, R. (2007), 'More labels, fewer refugees: remaking the refugee label in an era of globalization', *Journal of Refugee Studies*, 20(1): 172–92.

Zolberg, A., A. Suhrke and S. Aguayo (1989), *Escape from Violence: Conflict and the Refugee Crisis in the Developing World*, Oxford: Oxford University Press.

INDEX

EU representative:
Easy Access System Europe
Mustamäe tee 50, 10621 Tallinn, Estonia
Gpsr.requests@easproject.com

www.ingramcontent.com/pod-product-compliance
Lightning Source LLC
Chambersburg PA
CBHW071023280326
41935CB00011B/1469